ENDORSEMENTS

For most of my life (until I entered my late 50s), I never battled depression, not even once. I hardly knew what the word "depression" meant. Then it hit me...even me. My story is complicated, but I can tell you that I know what it's like to hit rock bottom and to think you will never enjoy sunlight again. Thankfully, I made it through, and now my depression is completely gone. In his new book on depression, Jeff Zaremsky is very wise pointing people to Dr. Neil Nedley and to his work. I know Dr. Nedley well, and there is no doubt that his expertise and his program (which I went through) helped pull me out of the pit. Jeff's focus on closely examining the lives of different people in the Bible who also struggled with depression is also extremely valuable. I highly recommend *Depressed People of the Bible*. It's a winner, and may be the key you need to unlock healing in your life, or in the life of someone you care about.

STEVE WOHLBERG
Speaker/Director, White Horse Media
Author of *Help for the Hopeless: My Escape from Insomnia, Mind-Altering Medication, Dark Depression* and *Mental Torture*

Jeff cleverly structures this book by delineating ten risk factors for depression, then showing how prominent Bible characters fell prey to them, ultimately rising to joy by embracing powerful, simple, timeless health principles. Stuffed with the practical, sensible kind of spirituality we so need to thrive and grow to our fullest potential, this readable, entertaining, wisdom-rich book should be on every night stand.

JENNIFER JILL SCHWIRZER
Licensed counselor, public speaker
Director of Abide Counseling Network; www.Abide.Network
Author of *13 Weeks to Peace, 13 Weeks to Love, 13 Weeks of Joy,*
and many others

In Jeff Zaremsky's new book on depression and biblical characters, he outlines a condition of the soul as old as humankind and the Bible. He has presented a biblical worldview of depression resolved in the hope of Scripture and turning the reader back to the heart of God. In this book the reader will discover that characters such as Moses and David are much like them. There is hope and healing for those whose feet are mired in the well of despair. Read and be impelled out of depression and into new life and purpose in God.

DR. THOMAS RICHARD GARDNER
President, Restored Life Ministries
Author of *Beyond the Wilderness, Healing the Wounded Heart,
The Healing Journey,* and many others

DEPRESSED PEOPLE

OF THE BIBLE

Freedom from a Cave of Depression to the Light of Life

JEFF ZAREMSKY

© Copyright 2021–Jeff Zaremsky

All rights reserved. This book is protected by the copyright laws of the United States of America. This book may not be copied or reprinted for commercial gain or profit. The use of short quotations or occasional page copying for personal or group study is permitted and encouraged. Permission will be granted upon request. Unless otherwise identified, Scripture quotations are taken from the New King James Version. Copyright © 1982 by Thomas Nelson, Inc. Used by permission. All rights reserved. Scripture quotations marked KJV are taken from the King James Version. Scripture quotations marked CJB are taken from the Complete Jewish Bible, copyright © 1998 by David H. Stern. Published by Jewish New Testament Publications, Inc. www.messianicjewish .net/jntp. Distributed by Messianic Jewish Resources Int'l. www.messianicjewish.net. All rights reserved. Used by permission. Scripture quotations marked TLV are taken from the Tree of Life Translation of the Bible, Copyright © 2015 by The Messianic Jewish Family Bible Society. Used by Permission. All rights Reserved. All emphasis within Scripture quotations is the author's own. Please note that Destiny Image's publishing style capitalizes certain pronouns in Scripture that refer to the Father, Son, and Holy Spirit, and may differ from some publishers' styles. Take note that the name satan and related names are not capitalized. We choose not to acknowledge him, even to the point of violating grammatical rules.

DESTINY IMAGE® PUBLISHERS, INC.

P.O. Box 310, Shippensburg, PA 17257-0310

"Promoting Inspired Lives."

This book and all other Destiny Image and Destiny Image Fiction books are available at Christian bookstores and distributors worldwide.

Cover design by Eileen Rockwell

Interior design by Terry Clifton

For more information on foreign distributors, call 717-532-3040.

Reach us on the Internet: www.destinyimage.com.

ISBN 13 TP: 978-0-7684-5933-3

ISBN 13 eBook: 978-0-7684-5934-0

For Worldwide Distribution, Printed in the U.S.A.

1 2 3 4 5 6 7 8 / 25 24 23 22 21

CONTENTS

Introduction

THERE IS HELP FOR THE HOPELESS

BY STEVE WOHLBERG

...When I sit in darkness, the Lord will be a light to me (Micah 7:8).

UNTIL I ENTERED MY 50S, I HAD NEVER BEEN DEPRESSED IN my entire life—not even once. Then the summer of 2017 arrived, and my world suddenly became a total mess. I didn't see it coming. My nightmare started when I lost my ability to sleep at night, or even to take naps during the day. The joy of living quickly vanished. In sheer desperation, I started taking powerful pharmaceutical drugs. Lorazepam was the worst. Then I became severely depressed. Gazing at myself in the mirror, I discovered that all light had left my eyes. My appetite vanished, and I was getting thinner and thinner. My future looked as dark as midnight. I even had suicidal thoughts, which were completely abnormal for me. I felt helpless, hopeless, and alone.

Today, that awful ordeal is over. What a relief! After my complete recovery, I decided to share my story publicly by writing a small booklet entitled, *Help for the Hopeless*. I was amazed at the response. So many contacted me saying that they could fully relate to my struggles. They were also encouraged to know that they were not alone, and that there was hope for them, too.

Rest assured there is hope for you as well.

Jeff Zaremsky's new book, *Depressed People of the Bible,* gives you tools that can help you. Jeff also connects his readers with the work of Dr. Neil Nedley, a brilliant physician in California who has become an expert in helping people find their way out of dark holes. During my depression, I attended Dr. Nedley's Depression and Anxiety Recovery Program. What a wonderful program that was! With my own eyes I saw my fellow participants experience miraculous transformations. One young lady was like a zombie when the program started. She hardly spoke. She just stared blankly. At the end of only ten days, she was smiling and laughing. It was a miracle!

Dr. Nedley's program is comprehensive. Participants are placed on a healthy diet. We exercise daily, drink lots of water, attend lectures, talk to counselors, are given full-body massages, listen to classical music, and experience the joy (or shock!) of intense hot-then-cold water treatments, which can almost bring the dead back to life.

But one of the most significant parts of Dr. Nedley's program is the bloodwork. Samples of our blood are sent to labs, which allows Dr. Nedley's trained eye to see exactly what's going on inside our brains. When he saw my blood results, Dr. Nedley knew exactly what supplements I was low in and needed to take. It's amazing how the combination of carefully prescribed natural supplements literally change my life. Wow! What a journey!

During my depression, one of the things that helped me so much was learning to rely on the healing promises of the Bible. Scriptures like the following became my lifeline to hope and sanity:

- *I have loved you with an everlasting love...* (Jeremiah 31:3).

- *Call upon Me in the day of trouble; I will deliver you, and you shall glorify me* (Psalm 50:15).

- *I will restore health to you, and heal you of your wounds, says the Lord* (Jeremiah 30:17).

- *Come to Me...I will give you rest* (Matthew 11:28).

- *Peace I leave with you, My peace I give to you...* (John 14:27).

- *I will never leave you nor forsake you* (Hebrews 13:5).

- *Fear not, I will help you* (Isaiah 41:13).

Night after night, day by day, I would think about those Bible promises, and others like them. I also searched my heart and confessed every wrongdoing I could think of. I prayed and prayed.

Truly, God's promises became my life. In my darkest days, I also learned a most valuable lesson: Whenever my mind, feelings, head, or heart tells me I'm hopeless, it's not true at all.

Those thoughts are lies.

I learned to rely on what God says, not what I think.

The struggles of certain people in the Bible also greatly encouraged me, such as what happened to the prophet Elijah. He became so depressed he wanted to die. I could totally relate. I felt like that too. Many times I felt the pressing temptation to end my life. But, thank God, He gave me strength to keep on going. Finally, the fog lifted, and my brain snapped back to normal. How grateful I am! Those dark days are now behind me.

The information in *Depressed People of the Bible* will help you recover your life, too.

I'm so glad that Jeff Zaremsky wrote this book!

STARTING LINE TO HEALING

Depression is experienced globally. It finds its way into every type of person on this planet. Cases of depression have been steadily increasing, and the average age of people who are affected by it is getting lower. That is in spite of us having more leisure, more prosperity, more conveniences, and more entertainment than at almost any other time in earth's history.

Neither wealth, popularity, influence, position, career, upbringing, nationality, race, nor even religion escapes its clutch. I don't have to tell you that, you know that from firsthand experience, don't you? You have seen it, you know someone who is affected by it, you have lived it, you have experienced it. Rich and poor, young and old, strong and weak, have all experienced depression. It is also an ancient problem.

Depression has been around for a long time. The Bible records examples of depression from thousands of years ago, even among its key personalities. Unlike many of the bibliographies and historical writings of today, the Bible tells us not only the good, but also the bad and difficult experiences of its star characters. Because of the willingness of the Bible to tell us the vulnerabilities of people, it is uniquely positioned to give us realistic examples to study. This honest writing of their struggles is very helpful for you and me. All of the people mentioned in this book experienced situations and difficulties like you and I have experienced. We will use their lives as case studies to help us understand ourselves. Sometimes it is easier to look at someone else's situation than it is to look at our own. Thus, by looking at their lives we will find lessons to assist us with our lives. We will see ourselves in their experiences and we will be able to learn from their victories and mistakes.

There is hope. There is a way out of depression. My good friend Steve Wohlberg can testify to that. During the summer of 2017, Steve was at the height of his career, popular in his field, with a loving wife and wonderful children. Steve had strong faith in God and was living a healthy lifestyle surrounded by nature and the beauty of North Idaho. Then, suddenly, depression attacked and overwhelmed him—for a time. Steve found a way out of the depression by contemplating the lives of people in the Bible and by going to a Nedley Depression and Anxiety Recovery Program at Weimar Lifestyle Center in California. In his encouraging book, *Help for the Hopeless,* Steve tells his own story.

Dr. Neil Nedley, who developed that program, is not a psychiatrist or a psychoanalyst. He is a trained internal medicine physician. Dr. Nedley was trained to not merely treat symptoms but to find out the cause. Many of his internal medicine patients suffered from depression, so he decided to research the causes of depression. When the cause can be stopped or reversed, the symptoms go away.

Dr. Nedley realized that depression is not a disease, but a set of symptoms. Instead of treating depression as a disease, he worked on finding out how to eliminate the causes. This led him to develop the Nedley Depression and Anxiety Recovery Program. Thousands of people have been helped through that program.

In the book *Depression: The Way Out,* Dr. Neil Nedley identified "10 hits" of depression. According to Dr. Nedley, an individual needs four or more of these ten hits occurring simultaneously in his/her life over a period of time for them to develop depression. As long as we keep our hits under four, we will not suffer from clinical depression. We may still experience situational depression for a temporary time even if our hit level is under four. This is very encouraging since we are able to control most of them and thus keep our hit levels under four.

After we identify and understand the ten hits, we will begin to compare the lives of people in the Bible who suffered from situational or clinical depression and try to identify what "hits" they might have had. From that, we will also be looking at what they did or should have done to avert or emerge from the depression. Often the Bible does not give us enough information to be able to identify if those people in the Bible were actually experiencing a depression hit. The plan is to identify with them and then to use their experiences as mirrors to see what areas in our personal lives are similar to theirs and learn from those experiences—not to become their judges or psychoanalysts.

Some of the people we will be reading about successfully came out of the depression, others did not. Some, such as Moses, Elijah, Jonah, Jeremiah, Judas, and King Saul, were even suicidal (or at least asked God to take their lives or wished they were never born). Other people we will be looking at include Naomi, David, Martha and Mary, Ahab, and even one very surprising Individual.

We will also be hearing modern-day stories of deliverance from depression, stories that you will be able to relate to, stories that will encourage you and give you hope that you also can successfully conquer depression.

Linda drove her car at top speed right into an overpass trying to kill herself. Subsequently she was put on medications and was approved for Social Security Disability for depression. Barbara became so depressed she could no longer function at work. In addition to work, it affected her social life, thoughts, attitude, eating habits, and sleeping. Do any of those circumstances that Linda or Barbara experienced sound familiar to you? Linda is my mother, Barbara is my wife. I have seen loved ones such as these and others be healed and recover from depression. You can also.

A great aunt on my father's side of the family committed suicide before I was born. Her sister, my grandmother, suffered from depression and was on medication for it. The family feared my grandmother might follow her sister's actions, but fortunately she did not. She lived to be 101 years of age. As mentioned, my mother was suicidal and depressed. My parents divorced when I was 12.

When I was 15, I ran away from home and was homeless for several months before moving in with my grandparents. Thus, I will most likely always have with me the two unchangeable depression hits, genetic and developmental. But thus far, thank God, I have not suffered from clinical depression. My wife has, and I have had depressed thoughts, but I believe it has been an intentional following, by God's grace, the principles brought out in this book that have kept me from experiencing clinical depression. It is these principles that helped my mother, my wife, and many others gain victory over depression.

It is my hope and prayer that this book will help you, and those whom you love, to be able to come out of depression and stay out of depression.

Author's Disclaimer: This book is not intended for diagnosis or treatment of depression. It is a biblical reflection on people throughout the Scriptures who dealt with depression and how God carried them through it to healing and purpose.

2

DEPRESSION TEST

IN THE VIDEO SERIES DEPRESSION RECOVERY,[1] DR. NEDLEY quotes from the psychiatric Bible describing the nine symptoms of depression. Not everyone who experiences depression has all nine symptoms; they may only have five or six. They include: fatigue, deep sadness, apathy, agitation, sleep disturbances, weight or appetite changes, lack of concentration, feelings of worthlessness, and morbid thoughts.

The following questions are designed to help you self-identify if you think you suffer from depression or know someone who does. This is not meant to be an official diagnosis.

1. Are you or your loved one experiencing deep sadness or a feeling of emptiness nearly every day for the past two weeks or more?

2. Are you experiencing a markedly diminished interest or pleasure in all or nearly all activities for the past two weeks or more?

3. Have you experienced a decrease or increase in appetite?

    a. Or if your weight is 100 pounds have you gained or lost 5 pounds or more?

    b. If you weigh 150 pounds have you gained or lost 7 pounds or more?

    c. If you weigh 200 pounds have you gained or lost 10 pounds or more?

4. Do you sleep more than you used to?

    a. To total more than 40 minutes per day?

    b. Or are you more sleepy in the day time and feel like taking naps frequently? (if you are not used to napping)

5. Or sleep less than you used to?

    a. To total more than 40 minutes shorter sleep duration?

    b. Or difficulty falling asleep or earlier awakening?

6. Have you been more agitated or irritated with yourself or others? Or you would qualify for a yes to number 5 if your physical movements have been slower than they used to be.

7. Have you experienced fatigue?

8. Have you experienced feelings of worthlessness? Have you experienced feelings of excessive or inappropriate guilt?

9. Have you experienced a diminished ability to think or concentrate? Especially if there is a difficult decision to make? Do you experience a decrease in your ability to make sound decisions?

10. Do you have recurrent thoughts of death? Or have you seriously considered harming someone else? Have you seriously considered suicide? Have you attempted suicide?

Depression is a constellation of symptoms, not a disease. A diagnosis of depression is only a diagnosis of symptoms, not the real problem. A runny nose is a symptom, not a disease. If we just treat symptoms, you might be prescribed a tissue to help your runny nose. But if we really wanted to treat the problem, the bacteria that is causing the nose to run, then we would work on attacking the bacteria. Once the bacteria is killed, the runny nose stops. Not the other way around. Too often we try to treat depression, when that is only the symptom. It is better to find out what hits are putting the person over the top and treat them, then the depression will stop.

Depression is disabling, but it does not have to be a permanent disability. A person with no legs does not have the ability to walk independently. They have a dis-ability. Thankfully many people without legs can still be mobile with the use of prosthetic legs, wheel chairs, etc. But their original legs will never grow back, they can never be "healed" in the sense of regaining their own flesh and blood legs. Depression is different; depression can go away. A person with the symptoms of depression can be healed of those symptoms and have the depression go away. Their original cheerfulness and productivity can come back. It has happened to many people and it can happen for you also.

Too often depression is thought of as an incurable disease or irreparable disability. It is used as an excuse. Hope is lost, and healing becomes that much harder. A person with that type of thinking resolves themselves to the lie that this is how it is going to be forever. They then expect everyone around them to accept as normal their mood swings, verbal attacks, negative outlook, nasty behavior, and unsociable conduct. But those harmful thoughts and actions are not healthy for the person or anyone else. Nor do they have to be permanent. There is hope, there is healing.

When we keep our depression triggers under four, the symptoms of clinical depression leave, and the person returns to who they really are.

The 10 hits that Dr. Nedley identifies as being depression triggers are:

1. Genetic; 2. Developmental; 3. Lifestyle; 4. Circadian Rhythm; 5. Addiction; 6. Nutrition; 7. Toxic; 8. Social/Complicated Grief; 9. Medical Condition; and 10. Frontal Lobe.

1. Genetic hit category: Family history of depression or suicide in a first-degree relative.

2. Developmental hit category: Early puberty in girls (beginning menstruation by age 11 years or younger), history of depression in adolescence, not being raised by both biological parents, sexual abuse, and being raised or living with someone who is an alcoholic or drug addict.

3. Nutrition hit category: Low dietary tryptophan; low omega-3 fat intake; low folic acid intake; low vitamin B intake; diet high in cholesterol, saturated fat, and sugar; and marked anorexia and weight loss.

4. Social hit category: Absence of social support, negative or stressful life events, low social class, being raised by grandparents, and immediate family member being an alcoholic or drug addict.

5. Toxic hit category: High lead levels; high mercury levels; high arsenic, bismuth, or other toxin levels; or high risk of exposure to these toxins.

6. Circadian rhythm hit category: Regular insomnia, routinely sleeping more than 9 hours per day or less than 6 hours per day, and not having regular hours for sleeping and eating.

7. Addiction hit category: Use of alcohol, cigarette or tobacco use, heavy caffeine use, recreational drug use (including marijuana), daily use of benzodiazepines, or chronic narcotic use for more than 30 consecutive days.

8. Lifestyle hit category: Not on a regular aerobic exercise program, not regularly exposed to daylight or a medical-grade light box for at least 30 minutes a day, and rarely breathing fresh air.

9. Medical condition hit category: Hepatitis C, recent head injury, stroke, heart disease, terminal cancer, Parkinson's disease, uncontrolled diabetes, severe postpartum stress, premenstrual tension syndrome, inadequately treated thyroid disease, lupus, inadequately treated adrenal gland disease.

10. Frontal lobe hit category: On low carbohydrate diet, on high meat or high cheese diet or eating lots of rich food, entertainment TV or movie addiction, entertainment Internet or chat Internet addiction, frequent sexual stimulation that activates right frontal lobe, regular exposure to syncopated rhythm music and/or videos, conscious suppression of frontal lobe activity, lack of regular abstract thinking, acting against one's conscience or known value system.

Of these 10 hits, only the genetic and the developmental ones are not reversible. Most of the other reversible hits are directly related to lifestyle choices.[2]

Many of the Bible people described in this book, such as Moses, Elijah, Jonah, David, Joseph, and others, had their life-changing experiences in a wilderness or cave type of setting when they were in the midst of a melancholy or even depressed state of mind.

Depression could be described as a cave with no opening and no light. It is cold. It is a dark place where no one else is allowed in. Time stops, and time does not matter. Depression is a state that no one else can understand or can relate to, and which no one else has experienced the way we are experiencing it. At least that is how it might feel.

But there are others who can relate, including some of the "big" names in the Bible. And the Lord is able to command the stone to be rolled away from the opening of the cave. He is able to say, "Let there be light" and light will shine on our face and path. He is able to awaken us and call us forth from the pit, and bring us back to life. He is able to instruct others to unwrap us and set us free. He is able to make us whole again.

Would you like to be made whole again? Would you like to see your loved one come out of the cave? Keep reading and you will be able to follow the path that many others have taken out of the cave and into the light.

PAUSE, PONDER, AND PROCEED

1. How many of the nine symptoms do you, or the person you are trying to help, currently have?

2. How many depression hits do you, or the person you are trying to help, have?

3. Which one would you like to start working on reversing?

4. Have you, or the person you are trying to help, ever thought of depression as an incurable disease or an unhealable disability?

5. Do you, or the person you are trying to help, want to be healed and return to how you really are?

6. Are you ready to start reading about people in the Bible who struggled with the same difficulties and thoughts that you have?

NOTES

1. "Depression & Recovery Session 1" with Dr. Neil Nedley; https://youtu.be/wymVfJgP5jI.

2. Neil Nedley, MD and Francisco E. Ramirez, MD, "Nedley Depression Hit Hypothesis: Identifying Depression and Its Causes," *American Journal of Lifestyle Medicine*, Vol. 10, Issue 6, November 1, 2016, pages 422-428.

3

MOSES

Part 1

THE BASKET CASE

MOSES LIVED 120 YEARS. HIS LIFE CAN BE BROKEN DOWN into three main sections, each being forty years in length. The first forty years he spent in Egypt.

Moses started off life as a basket case (pun intended). And at one point he was even suicidal (we will get to that in a bit). As Moses' mother saw babies all around her being killed and thrown to the crocodiles, we cannot begin to imagine the feelings of real fear, anxiety, concern, and grief that flowed through the umbilical cord and mother's milk during Moses' time in his mother's womb and while being breastfed. That was just the beginning.

We can't imagine the separation anxiety and abandonment Moses experienced when he was separated from his mother, father, sister, and brother when Jochebed was done weaning him.

Then there is the trauma of assimilation into a new family and a new culture, with the pressures of being in the royal family, living in a glass bowl, having to measure up, live up to a certain standard, not to mention the intense competition for the throne and positions around the throne.

All of that and so much more influenced the early childhood of Moses. It is probably fair to say there was a good chance Moses experienced genetic and developmental hits. Moses started off life with two out of ten on the hit list. Which does not leave much wiggle room, and satan made sure he didn't get it.

In adulthood, Moses was faced with the huge dilemma of feeling a part of two worlds. He related to his adopted family of the Pharaoh's daughter and of Egyptian culture, but was also drawn to his biological Jewish heritage of the slaves. To whom would he align his future? What were the risks? What would be the consequences of one over the other? The nagging conviction to align with the slaves was no doubt a very difficult one to shake and to accept. Social hit struck him pretty hard here, not knowing who to trust as his support group, not having anyone around who could help him understand his feelings or relate to the inner conflict he was experiencing, or to give him advice on which direction to take.

Then there were the bouts of frontal lobe hits attacking him whenever convenient to put him over the four threshold as he tried to decide what his conscience was really telling him, and as he battled to do what was "right." Should he stand against the throne, align with slaves, and help them rebel against his adopted family, their captives? Many times the thoughts must have run through his head, "Is that the right thing to do? Am I crazy or what?"

At the age of 40 Moses decided he should suffer affliction with the people of God. He took matters into his own hands and killed an Egyptian. This murder must have plagued Moses' conscience with regret throughout his life. This murder did not bring about the acceptance of the Israelites that he desired. Instead of acceptance, *"they did not understand"* (Acts 7:25) him and as a result of this act, Pharaoh understood him too well and *"sought to kill Moses"* (Exodus 2:15). Moses had to flee from Egypt to wander, literally, all alone, rejected by all—but God was there to meet him.

Have you been in situations where you were called to make some very hard decisions and you had no one to talk to who could relate to your dilemma or who would be a safe confidant?

Can you relate to Moses' conflict of knowing the "right" action probably will not go well and in the end will cost you your current lifestyle, possibly your family, your job, or even your life?

The pressure must have been exorbitant as Moses battled with the decision to no longer *"be called the son of Pharaoh's daughter. He chose being mistreated along with God's people rather than enjoying the passing pleasures of sin"* (Hebrews 11:24-25 CJB). How did he handle such pressure? What kept him from falling into depression at this point? *"He had come to regard abuse suffered on behalf of the Messiah as greater riches than the treasures of Egypt, for he kept his eyes fixed on the reward. By trusting, he left Egypt, not fearing the king's anger; he persevered as one who sees the unseen"* (Hebrews 11:26-27 CJB).

Have you made decisions or mistakes in your life that caused you to be misunderstood and rejected? Have your actions caused you to lose your job, home, family, or friends? Moses found his solace in the wilderness. Many people in this book found their peace with God and themselves in the wilderness. It is in quiet time with God when we can hear Him speak to our souls. Your wilderness might be a walk in a nearby park, down by a waterside, or alone at night at the foot of your bed. Wherever it is, rest in His care and in His watchfulness over you.

Whatever stressful decisions you have to make in your life, face them with faith in God and count the reproach for the sake of Messiah greater than anything this world has to offer. Do not fear the consequences of the wrath of the "king." Keep your eyes on Him who is invisible.

PAUSE, PONDER, AND PROCEED

1. Did your biological mother have any extreme stress or drug abuse while you were in the womb?

2. Were you separated from your family for a long period of time in your childhood?

3. Do you have someone with whom you can speak and work out your troubles? Many might answer no, but think hard; have you spoken with anyone about any of your troubles in the last two days? If the answer is yes, then yes you do have at least one person with whom you can speak at least sometimes.

4. Have you ever made a mistake that caused people to turn on you?

5. Have you ever been fired, divorced, or asked to leave a group?

6. Confess to God any mistakes you might have made and accept His forgiveness.

7. Accept by faith any and all consequences that have come to you because of other people's wrong choices or because of your own mistakes.

8. Choose to leave the problems of the past behind and move forward.

9. If you are in a situation between making a right choice that could have negative consequences, and a wrong choice that could put off trouble for a short time, choose to make the right choice. Choose to trust God with the consequences of that right choice.

Part 2

PEACE AND QUIET

MOSES' MEMORIES OF HIS MISTAKES, LOSS OF OPPORTUNITY to fulfill his calling, and the loss of his families—Israelite and Egyptian—caused him tremendous grief and sorrow. In the midst of all of this, God gave Moses a new start and a family of his own.

God loves you and has a plan for you as well. You are as much loved by God as Moses was: *"I know the thoughts that I think toward you, says the Lord, thoughts of peace and not of evil, to give you a future and a hope"* (Jeremiah 29:11).

Change can be a huge factor in our lives that can set the stage for depression if not handled properly. The second forty-year period of time in Moses' life started with some very dramatic changes. Moses went from being a powerful prince with a promising future in a palace with great riches, to living in a tent in a wilderness as a shepherd, husband, and father of two sons.

This might have been the most peaceful time of Moses' life. Things were good, as long as he kept his mind on the present and didn't dwell on the familial losses, lost opportunities, and mistakes of the past, or on the suffering of the people he left behind.

The Bible does not tell us too much about this 40-year period of Moses' life. The Bible spends more time telling us about the times people experienced troubles and how God saw them through it than on the happy, peaceful times people experienced. This is for our encouragement to help us as we go through our tough times.

God got Moses' attention with a burning bush that would not be consumed. God spoke to him from that bush, telling him he would be used to deliver the children of Israel out of Egypt. Moses responded, "Who, me?" (Not exactly, but that is the gist of it.) This was not humility, this was insecurity. When God calls us to a position, He empowers us and provides all that is needed to fulfill that position.

At this point, another major change took place in Moses' life. He was 80 years old, content, happy, fulfilled, and settled. Then all of a sudden he had a huge responsibility thrown onto his shoulders and was told everything in his peaceful setting was going to change.

God convinced Moses of His calling and Moses surrendered his own plans and insecurities. This surrender made Moses the meekest man on the earth (see Numbers 12:3). Meekness is not weakness. Meekness is total surrender to God, which empowers us to be bold among all people. In this meekness, Moses bowed before God and took his sandals off in His presence. At the same time,

Moses was able to go before Pharaoh and demand that he let his slaves go free, even though Pharaoh was the most powerful person on the earth and had the authority to execute anyone on the spot. Moses did not just stand before this monarch once, he came before him ten times making his demand. That is the power of meekness. That is the power of surrender before God. That is the power of being secure in God's calling upon your life.

You might be facing a time of change in your life, possibly a career change, a change of living conditions (from a palace to a tent, from the city to the wilderness, from a prince to a shepherd), cultural change, changes in your social network; whatever it is, trust and rest in God.

PAUSE, PONDER, AND PROCEED

1. List the changes, both good and not so good, that have taken place in the last 3 months of your life.

2. Look at that list, one by one, and choose to be thankful for the good changes, and choose to accept the not-so-good changes.

3. Choose to leave the future with God, knowing and believing that the thoughts He thinks toward you are thoughts of peace and not of evil, to give you a future and a hope.

4. Choose to live in the present and focus on what God would have you do today.

5. Choose to surrender all your desires, plans, and strengths to the Lord, bowing humbly before Him.

6. Give the Lord all your fears and insecurities, and believe by faith that He has removed them from you.

7. Accept the Lord's boldness and strength to go forward and fulfill the purpose that He has for you today.

Part 3

SUICIDAL MOSES

THE LAST FORTY YEARS OF MOSES' LIFE WERE THE MOST exciting. This was when he was loved and adored by all—not! But those are the years he is best known for and admired for today. It is under the hardest times that the diamond is made, that the gold shines the brightest. It is in adversity when men and women of character are made.

Those last forty years were the years the first eighty years were preparing him for. He did not know his years in Pharaoh's court and the years as a shepherd in the wilderness were all training him for that very moment. You might be wondering, "What am I doing in this job? Why aren't I somewhere else, doing something else? Why am I living here? Why am I surrounded with 'these' people?" But God has a plan for you today and for your future. Where you are today, what you are doing today, and who you are with, are all part of God's plan for your future.

There are times in our lives when we are not loved and adored by all, maybe not even by those we are helping the most at the time. Sometimes it is not until much later, maybe not even until heaven, that our good actions are admired, appreciated, or recognized.

So when was Moses suicidal? This was within the second year of the people's deliverance from slavery. It was sometime after the second month of the second year in the wilderness, after the children of Israel left Mount Hor and began traveling toward the Jordan River to go into the Promised Land. Moses was about 81 years old. This was before it was decreed he would be wandering in the wilderness for forty years.

The people started to complain and a fire broke out among them. Some people died. Moses interceded for them and the fire stopped.

After that experience, the people complained about the manna God had miraculously provided for their sustenance. *"Moses was displeased"* (Numbers 11:10) and he began complaining to the LORD:

> *Why have You afflicted Your servant? And why have I not found favor in Your sight...? Did I conceive all these people? Did I beget them...? Where am I to get meat to give to all these people? ...I am not able to bear all these people alone, because the burden is too heavy for me* (Numbers 11:11-14).

Then came the line that revealed Moses' true state of mind. *"If you treat me like this, please kill me here and now—if I have found favor in Your sight—and do not let me see my wretchedness!"* (Numbers 11:15).

Moses begged God and basically said, "Kill me right now, if You really love me." That is a pretty wretched state of mind. What could have caused Moses to feel that way?

Up to that point things were good. The children of Israel had recently, a little over a year prior, been delivered from slavery and bondage. They had seen miracle after miracle. God was providing manna from heaven and water out of a rock, they received the Ten Commandments, they built a tabernacle, and now they were on their way to the Promised Land. It doesn't seem like it could have been better.

They experienced a mighty deliverance, their needs were met, they had prosperity, and they had a purpose and a plan. What more could a person want? But some people always seem to want to complain no matter what you do or what is happening. Maybe this took Moses by surprise. Maybe because things were so good, their complaining seemed even more ungrateful.

A few things were going on in Moses' life as well. Moses and the children of Israel were on the move. Moving is stressful. They were going on the promises of God, but still to an unknown place. Moving into an unknown future is stressful. Moses took the burden personally. Lots of responsibility is stressful. Moses took the complaining personally. Rejection is stressful.

Moses might have had a developmental hit from being raised by Pharaoh's daughter. His circadian rhythm might have been off if he was worrying each night about the move and what lay ahead. He certainly had a social hit if he felt he didn't have any social support. Plus he would have been stressed out if he thought it was his job to carry the burden of leading the people.

How did he get out of this depression? God told him to pick seventy people to help him, which he did. Moses' faith was strengthened when God reminded him His arm is not too short to save by providing the people quail until it came out their nostrils. Moses' focus was restored as he recognized once again that it was God who was really leading the people.

Perhaps you are going through a time of a low after a high, or a time of rejection after you were the one who helped "them" the most, or a time of stress based on work or other people's expectations. Maybe you are facing an unknown future and you are fearful and worried. Or possibly you don't have the support and help you need for the responsibilities you have.

Do not take on more than you can handle. Feel free to ask others to assist you. Whatever the circumstance, remember God is in control, He is almighty, He will never leave you nor forsake you, He loves you, He is the same yesterday, today, and tomorrow. He has a plan. Trust Him.

PAUSE, PONDER, AND PROCEED

1. Have you ever thought or do you now think that it would be better if God took your life?

2. Choose to believe that God has a purpose for your life.

3. Have people been unappreciative of all that you have done for them?

4. Choose to give the ungrateful grumblers and complainers over to God.

5. Write down responsibilities that are on your shoulders currently.

6. List the people to whom you are called to lead or be an example. It could be your young children, people at work, people in your congregation or social setting.

7. List people who would be able help you with your responsibilities. Even if you can't think of anyone initially, stay at it until you do, even if they can only help in a small way.

8. Choose to trust that God will provide the grace and help you need even if currently there are no humans who can.

9. Choose to accept your current situation, trusting that God is using it to develop your character for His kingdom and for a future purpose that He has for you.

MEEKNESS AND BOLDNESS

MOSES WENT FROM BEING SELF-CENTERED, TO NON-CEN-tered, to God-centered. That is a transition that would be good for all of us to experience. But it does not often come easily. While Moses was in the wilderness he heard God's calling on his life. In Hebrew, both "wilderness" and "word" share the same root, debar. In Hebrew, *wilderness* is מדבר *meed-bar*, and *word* is דבר *davar*. The similarity in the words could be because it is in the wilderness where we are able to hear God's Word. What you are experiencing now could be the wilderness where God wants to speak His Words into your heart.

Moses was rejected by Pharaoh and he was also rejected by his own people whom he was trying to help. But other than that suicidal moment, in forty years in the wilderness Moses was not deterred by the reactions of Pharaoh or the people. Because at this point in Moses' life it really did not matter what he thought or what others thought. The only thing that mattered to Moses was what God thought. And that, my friend, is the key to contentment.

God used Moses to deliver the people out of Egypt, to lead them to Mount Sinai and the presence of God Almighty, and to bring them to the edge of the Promised Land. Yet during the forty years wandering in the wilderness the people seemed to treat Moses with mixed emotions, sometimes following, other times rebelling. Moses' cousins staged a full-scale rebellion and an attempted coup to replace him. Even his brother and sister, Aaron and Miriam, questioned his leadership and his marital choice. They talked badly about him and to him. All of that pressure and rejection could have easily sent Moses into a depression—but he didn't go there, except once. Why?

Because he did not take it personally. Moses realized that they were the ones with the problem, not him. Since they were the ones with the problem, he did not pray, "Oh God please help me, no one likes me, everyone is mean to me, this is not fair. God punish them, teach them a lesson. Oh, why me, why me, always me." Moses did need help, what was happening to him was not fair, the burden was always falling on him, and at that point it seemed that no one loved him. But since he knew they were the ones with the problem, Moses interceded in prayer for God to forgive them and to help them with their problem. Again, he knew who he was in God. That was all that mattered.

It is not wrong to acknowledge that things are not fair and that we are being wronged. But if we stay in that mindset and don't look above ourselves, we can get stuck there. We don't want to get stuck there; it is not a happy place to be.

We would think after all Moses did and risked personally for the people they would be eternally grateful to him, but they weren't. Even his family wasn't. You may be tempted to get discouraged because your efforts have not been appreciated as they should. Your spouse, children, parents, boss, or friends may not always reciprocate positively to all you have done for them. You may think, "After all the diapers I changed..., after all I have done..., after all these years of hard work..., how dare they treat me this way, this is not fair, it is not right." You are right. It is not fair and it is not right. Unfortunately, sometimes it is what it is.

The reality is that people are jerks—and that includes you and me. People are going to reject us and disappoint us even after "all we have done for them." We are going to get hurt unjustly. That is the way it is in this world. It is not always intentional, but it does happen and it will continue to happen. This earth is not heaven. We are on our way to heaven. We are just passing through this dark period of earth's history.

Most of it is not personal. The reality is most of the time people, including you and me, are caught up in themselves and are not thinking about how their actions are affecting others. Yes, there are times when people are just out to get us. They are vengeful, hateful, and mean. But even then it is not because of us they are that way. They were that way before we came on the scene; we just happen to be in the middle of their target practice at the time. If they are rejecting you for no good reason, they are the ones with the problem, not you. God will take care of you. Since they are the ones with the problem, we should be praying like Moses did—for them.

I heard a story about someone who was being verbally abused. He said to the abuser, "If someone offers me a gift and I refuse it, to whom does the gift belong?" The abuser said, "To the one who offered him the gift." The abused person continued, "The gift of verbal abuse you are offering me, I refuse, thus it is yours."

As a child I was taught a rhyme, "Sticks and stones will break my bones, but names will never harm me." I have heard people respond to that by saying, words and name calling do hurt. Yes, but only if we listen to them and allow them to hurt us. We can ignore them. We can refuse the verbal abusive gift and leave it with them. That is what that rhyme was teaching children, choose not to let them harm you.

Another rhyme was, "I am rubber, you are glue, what you say will bounce off me and stick to you." It really can be that way, if we choose not to accept their verbal abuse. God has given us the amazing power of choice. Exercise it; use it.

In addition to choosing not to listen to people's negative words, we can also choose to not be around people who continue to try to abuse us with their negative words. Separating yourself from the verbal abuser might be difficult, but it might also be necessary.

Don't take another's problems and make it your depression. Leave it with him or her. Trust that God will take care of you. Remember, it is only what God thinks of you that counts, and He loves you. After rejecting to listen to their negative talk, fill your mind with God's promises. Read His Word, listen to godly music, and repeat Bible promises out loud.

Sometimes God is using these situations for our good and we don't even know it.

I believe God has a greater good in store for you and me, and no one else can stop that from coming our way. We can blow it and reject what God has in store for us, but no one else can take it from us or stop God from giving it to us. How can we blow it and reject it? Through sin and unbelief. How do we get rid of the sin and unbelief?

- *If we confess our sins, He is faithful and just to forgive us of all sins and cleanse us from all unrighteousness* (1 John 1:9).

- *They overcame him by the blood of the Lamb and the word of their testimony...* (Revelation 12:11).

- *"Lord, I believe; help my unbelief!"* (Mark 9:24).

The formula for getting rid of sin and unbelief in Moses' day, actually from Adam and Eve until the Messiah, was to confess the sin to God, bring a spotless lamb to the sanctuary, lay your hands upon it, and believe your sin transferred to the lamb. Then you had to cut the lamb's throat, sacrifice the lamb, and accept its death in place of your death. The lamb received your punishment on your behalf.

That was pretty horrible for the lambs, but it shows us how horrible sin is and how sin affects God Himself, for He became the Lamb of God who takes away the sin of the world. After you sacrificed the lamb, God accepted the substitute and you were forgiven. At that point you could ask God to give you faith and power not to do it again.

Today it is similar, only that we accept the Messiah's sacrifice on our behalf instead of sacrificing our own lambs.

Pause, Ponder, and Proceed

Today is your life more self-centered, non-centered, or God-centered?

1. If you could not honestly say God-centered, pause right now in your own quiet "wilderness" and ask God to reveal Himself to you and to re-center your life. (Brace yourself, it might mean a Moses experience awaits you, but it will be worth it.)

2. Say out loud, "I choose to accept that in this life, on this earth, there will be ups and downs, and I choose to accept God's care for me in spite of the difficulties here. I choose not to accept the negative, hurtful abuse by others. I choose to accept God's love for me."

3. If it has upset you that you were not fully appreciated for the good you have done, then choose to be only concerned with the appreciation that God gives, not humans.

4. If your prayers have been more about God helping you than God helping others, ask God to give you His heart and His love for others.

5. Pray for three people, in particular people with issues such as those who have been so wrapped up in themselves that they have not appreciated what you have done for them. (Don't just pray about them, pray FOR them, for their benefit, for their welfare.)

6. If there is a sin in your life—a known wrong that you consciously and rebelliously hold on to—that is blocking God from being able to truly bless you, ask God to forgive you for that sin. It could be anger, insecurity, fear, bitterness, negativity, being unthankful, grumbling, complaining, or a whole host of other things the Bible speaks out against. After you confess it, accept His forgiveness because of the sacrifice of the Messiah. Then ask Him to fill you with His Spirit to empower you not to fall for those sins again.

Part 5

SUMMARY OF MOSES' LIFE

MOSES' LIFE WAS DIVIDED INTO A TRIFECTA OF THREE FORty-year sections. In the first forty-year section, Moses was everything—a "divine" child miraculously drawn out of water, destined to sit on the throne or at least close to it. Within this time he had "messianic" intentions of delivering the people by his own hand. During the second section, Moses was nothing, a failure, an outcast, a murderer, a simple shepherd with a small family. He even told God he was unfit for God's calling. In the third forty-year section, God is everything. Moses surrendered all to God and followed His lead.

In summary, the trifecta of Moses' life was: Moses is everything; Moses is nothing; God is everything. This third section is the section we want to be in all the time.

Being everything and being nothing are really two sides of the same coin. Both pride and insecurity can lead to depression: *"Pride goes before destruction, and a haughty spirit before a fall"* (Proverbs 16:18).

Both pride and insecurity are based on selfishness. Both focus on self and how "I" compare with others. Both focus on self-esteem. What is self-esteem? It is a self-estimate. It is the estimate or value that we put on ourselves. What is that estimate based on? It is based on what we have allowed society to tell us is important or not. Do we measure up to others? Do we measure up to their standards? When we think we measure better than others, we are proud; when we think we measure lower, we are insecure and cast down. Either way, the focus is on self, what we say or society says about us. Thus, we are the focus and that is the problem. The Bible says, *"...they, measuring themselves by themselves, and comparing themselves among themselves, are not wise"* (2 Corinthians 10:12).

That is a clear description of self-esteem. Thus, when we make self-esteem the basis of our security, we are not wise.

Life is not about us, it is about God. God is everything. Our estimate is not based on what we think about ourselves or on what others think about us. It is based on what God thinks of us and what He paid for us. He paid His life for us, thus we are of the highest estimate in His eyes. That estimate will not change, because it is not based on you, what you can or can't do. It is based on what He already did. What we need is not a high self-esteem, but a God-esteem. God esteems you very highly, as highly as He esteems Himself.

The Bible describes us in two polar opposite ways that balance each other out and give us a true estimate of our abilities and value:

- *...Without Me you can do nothing* (John 15:5).

- *From dust you are, and to dust you shall return* (Genesis 3:19).

- *...All our righteousnesses are filthy* [menstrual] *rags...* (Isaiah 64:6).

- *...There is none who does good, no, not one* (Psalm 14:2-3).

That is a pretty clear and dismal but very accurate description of our lives. We can deny those realities and try to puff ourselves up, but that would not be wise. Even worse, it would set us up for a fall.

At the same time the Bible says:

- *I can do all things through Messiah who strengthens me* (Philippians 4:13 TLV).

- *It is God who works in you both to will and to do for His good pleasure* (Philippians 2:13).

- *For God so loved the world He gave His only begotten Son, that whosoever believes in Him should not perish but have everlasting life* (John 3:16).

- *Behold what manner of love the Father has bestowed on us that we should be called children of God!* (1 John 3:1).

- *We love Him because He first loved us* (1 John 4:19).

It is balancing those two groups of texts that we can discover our true worth. In ourselves we are nothing, worthless. Yet by God's grace, because of His great love for us, we are very valuable. A Bible verse that combines both concepts is Galatians 2:20 (CJB):

When the Messiah was executed on the stake as a criminal, I was too; so that my proud ego no longer lives. But the Messiah lives in me, and the life I now live in my body I live by the same trusting faithfulness that the Son of God had, who loved me and gave himself up for me.

It is only when we realize our true nothingness that we can truly see God. Not the insecure nothingness of Moses in the wilderness, saying "I can't do anything," but a nothingness that sees itself as totally dependent upon the God of the universe who can do everything, even through us.

The Bible describes an angel called lucifer—later called satan or the devil—whom God created and imbued with great beauty and talents:

You were in Eden, the garden of God; every precious stone was your covering.... You were perfect in your ways from the day you were created, till iniquity was found in you. By the abundance of your trading you became filled with violence within, and you sinned; therefore I cast you as a profane thing out of the mountain of God; and I destroyed you, O covering cherub.... Your heart was lifted up because of your beauty; you corrupted your wisdom for the sake of your splendor; I cast you to the ground.... I brought fire from your midst; it devoured you, and I turned you to ashes upon the earth in the sight of all who saw you. All who knew you among the peoples are astonished at you; you have become a horror, and shall be no more forever (Ezekiel 28:13,15-19).

Then lucifer became so exalted in his own mind that he wanted to take God's throne.

> *How you are fallen from heaven, O Lucifer, son of the morning! ...you have said in your heart: "I will ascend into heaven, I will exalt my throne above the stars of God...I will ascend above the heights of the clouds, I will be like the Most High"* (Isaiah 14:12-14).

Because lucifer had too high self-esteem, that did not turn out good.

Humanity was originally created in the image of God, but through Adam and Eve's choice and our own, that has been broken. The Bible says our hearts are now naturally against God (Romans 8:7); thus our actions are self-based instead of God-focused. Since we now have a carnal nature, we all are constantly thinking about ourselves, esteeming ourselves, which either causes us to be proud, thinking we are better than others, or we are insecure, thinking we are worse than others. Either way, self-esteem is not the answer.

In God's battle to take us back from satan and to recreate His image in us, God placed His throne on the line. If satan won, he would have had God's throne. That is the value God placed on you and me. You are worth as much as God's throne. That is the estimate we need to accept for ourselves.

I can have an item—a car, house, painting, etc.—that I value immensely. I can think it is worth a lot. I may have even paid a lot for it. Yet, when I go to sell it, it is not me who really sets the price, but the buyer. I can set the price at what I paid for it and all I put into repairing it, but if no one will pay me that much, then it is not worth that much to anyone but me. A new baseball might only be worth a few dollars, a used baseball much less than that, but a used baseball that was used to hit a record-breaking homerun by some popular baseball player would be worth a lot to someone—not me, but to someone. Our worth is not based on what is naturally in us, but on the value that was paid for us. God paid the ultimate price for us.

Believing God's estimate of our worth to Him should make you feel very, very good.

You may have heard or read this illustration before, but it bears repeating. The estate sale of a wealthy art collector was attended by many rich buyers. The collection included rare and valuable paintings by world-renowned artists. As the auction began, the auctioneer started with a portrait of the art collector's son who had died at a young age. The art collector had painted the portrait himself. As the auctioneer started the bidding, no one was interested in the portrait. The auctioneer lowered the price and lowered the price; still no one offered anything for it. Soon the people started to call out for the auctioneer to bring out the pictures they had come to see and to leave that one for the end. But the auctioneer persisted, crying out, "Who will make an offer for the picture of the son?" Finally a groundskeeper for the estate who was fond of the art collector and his son offered what he could for it, thinking it would be a good reminder of his kind boss. With that purchase, the auctioneer ended the entire sale. Everyone in attendance was furious, but a lawyer for the estate stood up and said, "The will states that whoever buys the picture of the son receives the entire estate."

While that story might just be an illustration, it teaches a very important reality regarding our worth in God's eyes. If we have the Son, we have everything. Because of His sacrifice for us, we are adopted by God and become His children. Thus we become joint heirs of the kingdom of heaven. You and I have a great inheritance.

The victory over depression that Moses experienced was not from changes in his circumstances. It was not from situations in his life getting easier. It was not from people liking him more. His victory came through the choices he made inside. He chose to believe God's great love for him. He chose to receive his inheritance as God's child. As we choose the same, we also will have strength to cope with troubles that come our way as well as the problems from our past. I encourage you to make that choice right now.

Pause, Ponder, and Proceed

1. If you are tired of trying to build up your own self-esteem, and you are ready to accept God's estimate of you, say out loud, "I choose not to value myself based on what others think about me or what I think about me. I choose to estimate my worth based on the enormous price God paid for me, on the boundless love that He has for me. Thank You, God, for loving me so much that You gave Yourself for me."

2. If you are tired of trying to change your life without success and you want to accept God's power to change you, say out loud, "Lord God, I acknowledge that without You I can do nothing, but through You I can do all things. Live inside me and give me the power to be re-created in Your image."

4

JONAH—A CLASSIC EXAMPLE

JONAH WAS IN MANY WAYS LIKE YOU AND ME. HE WAS NOT called to lead the masses like Moses. He was simply called to tell his neighbor what God said. Isn't that what God asks of each of us?

We don't have any knowledge of Jonah's upbringing or lineage, so we do not know if hits one or two apply to him. But we do know enough about Jonah to identify at least a few possible hits and certainly at least one.

Our introduction to Jonah begins with God telling him to go to the large metropolitan city of Nineveh and to pronounce judgment upon the people because of their wickedness. Nineveh was a great, large, wicked city that was not even in the land of Israel.

Actually, it was quite far from Israel. Nineveh is still in existence today in the country of Iraq. It was not a Jewish city. The inhabitants were Gentiles. Jonah would be a foreigner with no national protection. He would be proclaiming to a city that did not believe in his God that his God was going to destroy them.

Jonah was called to a very dangerous assignment. You can probably think of some cities in the world that would fit this description. What would you do if God called you to go to one of them and tell them your God said they were going to be destroyed?

Jonah was not being asked to merely knock on his friendly neighbor's door and invite him to come to services. He was being commanded to go to a city filled with people who would have no problem killing him and leaving his body to be eaten by dogs. Not only was Nineveh a large and wicked city far from Jonah's homeland in another country, it also had not shown itself friendly to Jonah's nation or people. As a matter of fact, it had been very hostile to Israel and may have been responsible for the deaths or capture and enslavement of people Jonah knew, perhaps even relatives and loved ones of Jonah.

Jonah made a negative frontal lobe conscious decision to resist God's will. Rather than stepping out in faith, Jonah responded to his fears and went in the exact opposite direction of Nineveh. Jonah boarded a ship headed away from Nineveh toward Tarshish.

Instead of allowing Jonah to just run away from the Lord's service, God chased after him. Certainly God could have found someone else just as willing, or unwilling, as Jonah to go to Nineveh. This assignment was as much for Jonah's benefit as it was for Nineveh. In His love for Jonah, God was not going to let him out of this task. Much, if not all, of what we are called to do in life is for our benefit in the long run.

"The Lord sent out a great wind on the sea, and there was a mighty tempest on the sea, so that the ship was about to be broken up" (Jonah 1:4). The storm was so violent that strong, tough, experienced sailors feared for their lives. They cried out to their gods for help and cast their precious cargo overboard. Throughout all this turmoil and noise, Jonah was sleeping.

You might ask, "How on earth could Jonah be sleeping with all that noise from the wind, the rain, the thunder, the sailors crying out, and the sailors running around the ship hauling, dragging, and throwing large pieces of cargo around?" Jonah was in a deep depression and slept through it all in the dark bottom of the ship. Even if he did occasionally awaken and heard the storm and the sailors crying out, he might have thought to himself, "Good, if this ship sinks, at least this emotional pain will end."

Have you ever been so despondent that all you wanted to do was hide in a dark room or to isolate yourself from other people? Have you ever dipped so far down that you no longer cared about your life or the safety of others? Have you ever been so depressed that all you could do was sleep? If so, then you can relate to Jonah.

While we can't know all of Jonah's hits, we can surmise a few of them. He had a frontal lobe hit for resisting God's will. We can imagine him boarding the first ship heading out and getting on the ship in as quick a fashion as possible. In all that hustle, his circadian rhythm could easily have been out of whack. It is hard to imagine that ship having a fancy dining hall serving seven-course meals, so his nutritional balance could have been off. The ship's captain found him in the bottom hull of the ship, so he might not have been getting fresh air or sunlight. Can you think of any of the other hits or sub-hits Jonah might have been experiencing?

It is not one night's sleep or one insufficient meal that will cause a hit, but in these accounts of depressed people of the Bible we are only given the bare facts, not every detail of their lives. We are not analyzing these people from the Bible, we are just looking at possible scenarios so we can learn lessons for ourselves.

It is easy for us, in our self-denial, to think we only had one insufficient meal or only one night's bad sleep, when in reality it was several or many. If you ever had the thought, "That could never happen to me," that is a good example of self-denial.

The sailors asked Jonah to tell them something about himself and he answered in a very interesting way. Jonah replied, *"I worship the Lord God of heaven, who made the sea and dry land"* (Jonah 1:9 Contemporary English Version). This was not entirely a true statement. Jonah may have professed to worship the Lord and he might have done so when things were easy, but it is hard to truthfully say we are worshiping the Lord when we are in open disobedience to Him.

That applies to us as well. You may be praying, you may be reading the Bible, you may be singing songs of praise to God, you may be attending services, but if you are just going through the motions, you are not worshiping Him. Obeying Him would include allowing Him to live in your life, to empower you to live the life the Bible outlines. I am sure you have been gratified and enriched as you have seen Him bringing your life into harmony with the great teachings of Scripture. Seeing Him at work within us draws forth an attitude of worship.

Worshiping God also includes sharing God's love with someone else. God has called all of us to share His love with others. We become His hands to help, His feet to go, His mouth to share, His heart to love and care. We become His representatives, His ambassadors. What a privilege it is to be a representative of the Lord, the God of heaven, the Creator of the sea and the earth! If fear is the reason we are not moving out in faith, we can confess fear to the Lord, and He will remove it and replace it with His power. Regarding fear, God has given us a wonderful, powerful Bible promise: *"God has not given us a spirit of fear, but of power and of love and of a sound mind"* (2 Timothy 1:7). Accept God's victory over sin, worry, and fear right now; accept His power, His love, and His sound mind.

Jonah's understanding of God was not complete. When Jonah told the sailors he was running away from God, the sailors asked him what they could do to calm the storm. Jonah responded, *"Pick me up and throw me into the sea; then the sea will become calm for you. For I know that this great tempest is because of me"* (Jonah 1:12). Jonah's response showed he had not yet known of or experienced God's mercy and forgiveness. Jonah felt hopeless because he did not yet understand that God loved him personally and called him because He believed in him. Jonah saw the storm as a punishment, as opposed to being sent by a loving God who valued Jonah and did not want him to run away from Him. In this state of depression and without faith in a loving God, Jonah became suicidal and asked the sailors to throw him into the sea.

You might be going through a tempest in your life right now, and it might be in part because of choices you have made. If that is the case, God did not send the tempest to punish you, He allowed it to draw you to Him, to get you back on course. He allowed it not because He is angry, but because He loves you. He values you. He has a plan and a purpose for you.

Jonah seemed to have forgotten the accounts of Joseph and Job, that in every calamity God has a purpose and a plan. Because he did not remember these things, Jonah didn't realize this storm was actually for his good. Jonah must have forgotten how God accepted Jacob's, Moses', and David's repentance. He seemed to think the only way to stop the storm was by his death.

God did not want Jonah to die. He wanted him to repent of his sin and receive His forgiveness through the sacrifices offered in the Temple representing the Messiah's death. God wanted Jonah to accept the power of the Holy Spirit to take away his fear and cause him to be obedient to God's will for his life. If God's biggest interest was in accomplishing a task, proclaiming His judgment on Nineveh, He would have said, "If Jonah doesn't want to do my bidding and go to Nineveh, I will fire him or let him quit, let him run, let him be thrown overboard and drown, and I will get someone else who will do My will." But this story is not as much about God's concern about Nineveh—although God loved the people of Nineveh as well—as it is about God's love for Jonah.

God's calling and commands to us are not so much about accomplishing some action or fulfilling some duty. It is about God developing us into all that He wants us to be, a people who love and truly worship Him in heart, mind, and soul, in spirit, truth, and action. Whatever problem or duty you are called to face in your life, it is part of God's love for you, to grow you in His plan for your life. Do you believe that God loves you even when times are difficult, even when you are fearful and even when you are running from Him? Is there some area in your life where you need to receive God's forgiveness and love right now?

The sailors resisted throwing Jonah overboard as long as they could, but finally they gave in and tossed him into the sea. God did not let Jonah off the hook; He used a fish to catch Jonah. This is not your typical fishing trip, yet Jonah certainly had a whopper of a fish story to tell! God loves us even when we are being disobedient and running away from Him. God did not give up on Jonah or Nineveh—and He will not give up on you, me, or any of our loved ones.

A fish's belly is likely one of the darkest places. Jonah was there for three full days. His diet might have been limited and his circadian rhythm could very well have still been way off, but Jonah did something to bring himself out of the depression. He made a good frontal lobe decision. He began to accept God's love and cried out to the Lord. Like Moses alone in the wilderness, it was when Jonah was alone in the belly of a great fish that He really heard God calling out to him in love.

Maybe that is all you need right now to snap out of depression. Regardless of what you have done in the past, regardless of what others have done to you, and regardless of whatever fish's belly you are in right now, choose to believe that God loves you with an everlasting love. Accept His mercy and forgiveness. Accept His love demonstrated in the Messiah. Accept His power to move forward in obedience to His commands. If you are having a hard time choosing and believing such things, you can cry out to God, "Lord,

I believe, help my unbelief!" Or you can even cry out, "Lord, I don't believe, give me faith!"

God mercifully had the fish spit Jonah out on dry land. God, in His love for both Jonah and Nineveh, called Jonah to go to Nineveh. God had not forgotten how this calling would benefit both Jonah and Nineveh, so He reminded Jonah again of His command for Jonah to go and warn Nineveh. This time Jonah obeyed and got plenty of exercise and sunlight traveling all the way there. (I hope he had a chance to shower first. Smelling like fish food is not a recipe for a good first impression.)

Jonah began walking through the city proclaiming the message of God. The Spirit of God softened the Ninevites' hearts and they truly repented of their sins. What a powerful experience, and to think that Jonah was reluctant to go!

It would be interesting to see how many powerful experiences God has in store for us when we reject fear and accept God's power, love, and a sound mind.

As the city was repenting, Jonah found a nice spot on a hillside to watch the fireworks. This was going to be better than the destruction of Sodom and Gomorrah. Again, Jonah might have had family and friends who were killed or hurt by these people. He may have been looking forward to seeing God's revenge on them. But God did not destroy the city. He accepted their repentance. This *"displeased Jonah exceedingly, and he became angry"* (Jonah 4:1). Jonah began to accept God's love for him and became outwardly obedient, but he did not receive God's love to the point of being able to forgive and love others.

Jonah made a wrong frontal lobe decision and chose to be unhappy about the outcome and even angry at God. These negative thoughts threw Jonah over his four hit limit again and he again became suicidal, even to the point where he said, *"It is right for me to be angry, even to death!"* (Jonah 4:9). Anger and bitterness are very dangerous feelings to harbor.

Unfortunately, that is basically where the story ends for Jonah. God made another plea for him, but the Bible does not record Jonah's response. Fortunately, our stories are not over yet. God is still pleading with each of us, because He loves us.

The book of Jonah shows God's love for the city of Nineveh, which had caused so much heartache and pain to people who were following God. It also shows God's love to Jonah, who professed to be following God, but whose life did not always line up with that profession. The account of Jonah and the city of Nineveh might not have been primarily about God's love for either of them; it might be about God's love for you and me.

One of Jonah's big problems was bitterness. Two of the ways bitterness can manifest itself are anger and sadness. We can demonstrate the anger with hurtful words or actions, or we can hold the anger in and it can lead to sadness and depression. (This is not to say all depression is a result of holding onto bitterness.) Sadness and anger, as a result of bitterness, are two sides of the same coin. Whether you have allowed bitterness to become bursts of rage or self-pity and depression, you are the only one who can reverse the cycle by choosing to allow God to give you the ability to rise above the wrong that someone else has done.

Forgiveness is the recognition that God is stronger than the people who have wounded us. Forgiveness is the recognition that God is stronger than the past. Choosing to forgive—giving the frustration, anger, and hurt over to God—brings healing to us.

This does NOT mean you are saying people are right or directed by God to do evil. Actually, by forgiving we are calling out their wrong. We do not forgive people for doing good things. We only forgive people for doing bad things. Forgiveness does not mean, "It's okay." When someone does something wrong it is definitely not okay. Forgiveness does not mean we will or that they should "Forget it." No, both we and they need to remember and learn from that wrong so that it is not repeated against us or against anyone else.

Forgiveness does not mean punishment will not be enacted against the wrongdoer. The financial term "debt forgiven," indicates a debt is absolved and does not have to be repaid. This is a very erroneous application when it comes to biblical forgiveness. When a wrong is done to us, we can be forgiving and at the same time still expect the offender to pay back the debt, make the wrong right, lose privileges, be put in jail, or receive the appropriate discipline and punishment for the wrong they did. Even when God forgives us, He does not just wipe out the debt. The debt must be paid, and the payment required for sin is death. Not only the death of the Messiah, but a death on the part of the sinner—a death to sin, a death of the carnal nature of the sinner. We, our natural self, must die with the Messiah.

Then we become born anew, with new hearts, new minds, new thoughts, and new desires. God replaces our old self with the mind of Messiah; He fills us with His Holy Spirit and He writes

His laws into our hearts and minds. He changes us and empowers us. All things become new. We are not helpless victims. We are empowered overcomers.

When we choose to forgive, we are choosing not to hold on to anger and bitterness. When we forgive we are saying, "Someone did something wrong, they did something bad. I do not want them to ever do that again to me or to anyone else. That wrong might even entail some type of punishment against them. But I choose not to hold onto angry, bitter, hateful feelings against them because of their wrongs. I am not going to allow their wrong, hurtful choices to take away my joy. While I may have to bring criminal charges against them or take them to court or expect a compensation for the damage they did, I ultimately trust that God will deal with them. I choose to pray for them so that they can receive God's forgiveness and love. I am willing to allow God to use me to reach them if He so chooses. Their wrong is their problem. I choose not to let it become my problem. I choose to trust that even the negative physical, financial, or emotional effects that their wrong choices have had on me will be worked out together for good by God, who is bigger than all that happens in this world."

When we say, "I am willing to allow God to use me to reach them if He so chooses," we should add a word of caution. God did not call everyone who was hurt by the Assyrians to go to Nineveh. It is not always wise or safe or God's will to be the one to demonstrate God's love to the offender. There are many cases of employment, marriage, family, or social abuse where a codependent person remains in or goes back into the abusive situation under a pretense of forgiveness and an attempt to help the abuser. There are major differences between codependency and biblical forgiveness. Biblical forgiveness does not give someone a license to continue to hurt us. When there is danger of continued abuse, we may not be the one to be able to help them. Jonah was not called to "move in" with the people of Nineveh. He was called to warn them.

We do not have to wait for them to apologize before we forgive them. Remember, forgiveness is not letting them off the hook; it is an acknowledgment that what they did was wrong, that I am not going to allow their wrong to steal my peace, and that I will not respond with vengeance even if I have to make sure justice and punishment is enacted. Thus, forgiveness is more for our sake than for their sake. While our forgiving them does not release them from guilt or punishment, it does release us from anger and bitterness. If we wait until they apologize before we choose to forgive, then we are allowing them to decide when we will be released from the anger and bitterness that is destroying us. If we wait for them to apologize before we forgive, we are allowing them to control us, we are allowing them to continue to hurt us.

And what if they never apologize? What if they die before we do and never apologize? That would be the ultimate control wouldn't it. We would then be eternally stuck with anger and bitterness. That is why it is better to choose to forgive them right away. It is what God has done for us. *"God demonstrates his own love for us, in that the Messiah died on our behalf while we were still sinners"* (Romans 5:8 CJB). He forgave us even before Adam and Eve sinned, before we were even born. He is *"the Lamb slain from the foundation of the world"* (Revelation 13:8). As we accept His Spirit into our hearts, He will give us the ability to have pre-forgiveness toward those who hurt us.

Actually forgiving someone before they apologize can lead them to apologize. If we said to someone out of the blue, "I forgive you," their natural reaction would be, "What wrong did I do that you are forgiving me for?" Forgiving someone brings conviction to them that they did something wrong.

When they do apologize, our reaction should not be to say, "Oh, it's okay." We should be able to say, "I have already forgiven you." Under certain circumstances we could add, "This is going to be the consequence for doing that wrong.... How do you plan on changing so that it does not happen again?"

Do you need healing from feelings of hurt, bitterness, anger, or resentment so you can accept the gift of peace and trust in God right now? Just ask God to take away those harmful feelings of self-pity and sadness, or of hatred and revenge. Now choose to thank God that He has taken those hurtful feelings away. You can do this by *faith*. That means thanking God for removing those hurtful feelings whether you *feel* any different or not.

Now ask God to replace your feelings that are hurtful (that He has just taken away), with feelings of joy, peace, and contentment. Ask Him for a godly pity for those who hurt you. Also ask Him to give you faith that He will eventually work this out for good, knowing that in His time He will bring punishment for evil. Continue to ask for this every time those sad or angry feelings come back. Eventually they *will* stop disturbing your peace, and the Lord will have full control of this area of your life. He has done this for others; He can do it for you. People will soon start noticing the difference God is making in your life.

PAUSE, PONDER, AND PROCEED

1. If you are running away from doing something you know God wants you to do, ask God to forgive you, accept the Messiah's death for your mistake, accept His forgiveness, and accept His power to do what is right.

2. Can you think of a time when God allowed some "storm" to come into your life, and now you see it as God's loving attempt to try to get your attention and turn you to Him?

3. If you have been having a hard time believing that God loves you personally, say out loud, "Lord, I believe, help my unbelief." Or, "Lord, I don't believe, give me faith."

4. Have you ever gotten angry when you have seen God be merciful or beneficial to someone who was not nice to you or others? If so, and if you have not yet repented of that, thank God for showing mercy to them and claim His mercy upon yourself.

5. Have you ever been reluctant to forgive someone because you were taught to believe that forgiveness meant they would be released from accountability? Are you now seeing that true biblical forgiveness holds them accountable and also releases you from bitterness and anger?

6. If you are thankful for this true understanding of forgiveness, thank God right now.

7. If someone has hurt you and you have not yet forgiven them, choose right now, by God's power, to forgive them. (If you are still having a hard time doing that, ask God to give you the ability to forgive them as God has forgiven you.)

8. If you are in an abusive situation, ask God to give you the strength to get out of it.

Elijah—Highs and Lows

Elijah's story goes from a literal mountaintop experience down to a suicidal desire.

We are first introduced to Elijah in the Bible during a time of great apostasy in Israel. King Ahab allowed himself to be ruled by his wicked wife Jezebel. God called Elijah to tell the king that because of his sins it was not going to rain until Elijah said so. That took either chutzpah or tremendous faith, or maybe both.

God had Elijah hide out by the Brook Cherith where God used ravens to bring Elijah his daily rations. Eventually the drought got so bad the brook dried up. God sent Elijah to the home of a kind and faithful widow whose flour and oil miraculously never ran out. After some time, the widow's son died and Elijah witnessed God raise him from the dead.

Ahab had been sending out search parties to imprison or kill Elijah. All to no avail, they could not find him. After the three and half years of no rain, God called Elijah to return to Ahab and rebuke him again. Ahab was not happy. Ahab put all the blame on the messenger, calling Elijah a troubler of Israel. Elijah corrected the king, telling him it was the king's sins in forsaking the commandments of God that had caused the troubles. What boldness, what faith, what confidence, what chutzpah.

Elijah told Ahab to call all of Israel and all the king's pagan prophets to meet him on Mount Carmel. Ahab did what Elijah asked. Elijah spoke to all the people and asked, *"How long will you falter between two opinions? If the Lord is God, follow Him; but if Baal, follow him"* (1 Kings 18:21). Then Elijah turned to the pagan prophets and challenged them to a contest. Both were to build altars to their God, place a sacrifice on it, and whichever God answered by fire was the true God. Elijah let the pagan prophets go first. They built their altar, put their bull upon it, and began calling out to their god. From morning until late afternoon they danced around their altar, cutting themselves, and calling out to their god. But nothing happened. Elijah even mocked them saying, *"Cry aloud, for he is a god; either he is meditating, or he is busy, or he is on a journey, or perhaps he is sleeping and must be awakened"* (1 Kings 18:27).

Eventually they gave up and it was Elijah's turn. Elijah built an altar, put a slain bull on it, and dug a trench around the altar, and even though the drought had not ended, he had twelve buckets of precious water poured upon the bull, wood, and altar until the trench was filled with water. Then Elijah prayed and fire came down from heaven and burned up everything—the sacrifice, the wood, the water, even the stones. The people cried out, *"The Lord, He is God!"* (1 Kings 18:39). It must have been amazing to be there, but the account does not end there.

Elijah then prayed to God seven times and the Lord sent rain after three and half years of drought. God gave Elijah the strength to run before Ahab's chariot and lead him through the rain back to his palace. What a powerful experience. Elijah was on a high and no doubt expected a full revival to take place throughout the land. But his great disappointment sent him into a deep depression, even to the point of wishing he was dead.

When Ahab's wife, Jezebel, heard what had happened she was not a happy camper. She sent messengers out to Elijah stating that she would have him dead by the next day. Elijah, who had stood bravely for God for more than three and a half years, who had stood up to the king several times, who had been fed by God's ravens, who had seen God miraculously provide flour and oil for the widow, her child, and him, who had seen the boy die and then rise from the dead, who had seen fire come down from heaven and consume everything including the stones, now ran for his life in fear.

After running for a few days he was exhausted and accumulated several "hits" such as inadequate sleep and altered circadian rhythm, reduced nutrition, negative thinking, and possibly others. Elijah *"prayed that he might die, and said, 'It is enough! Now, Lord, take my life, for I am no better than my fathers!'"* (1 Kings 19:4). Elijah was suicidal, or at least wanted God to take his life; basically he wanted to be dead.

How did God respond to such a prayer? He sent an angel who gave Elijah some food and let him rest. Then the angel came back again and did the same thing. After resting and eating, Elijah journeyed to Mount Horeb, where God had given Moses the Ten Commandments.

Elijah was still depressed and he isolated himself for forty days.

When Elijah reached Mount Horeb, he went into a cave and slept overnight. God came to him and asked, "What are you doing here, Elijah?" Elijah was still bitter and presumptuous about how things should be working out. He declared, *"I have been very zealous for the Lord God of hosts; for the children of Israel have forsaken Your covenant, torn down Your altars, and killed Your prophets with the sword. I alone am left; and they seek to take my life"* (1 Kings 19:10). Notice all the fear and focus on self that Elijah expressed. Elijah had taken his eyes off God and placed them upon himself. He focused on his situation without taking God, or possibly other people, into consideration.

God responded by passing the cave with a strong windstorm, followed by an earthquake, followed by fire. But the Lord was not in any of those. Then God's still small voice called Elijah, asking again, *"What are you doing here, Elijah?"* (1 Kings 9:13). Again Elijah responded as before. It seems he had been rehearsing that line over and over again in his mind. A very dangerous practice which is far too common.

If you hold a small envelope in front of your face and focus on it, drawing it closer and closer to your eyes, you will eventually get to the point where this small envelope can obscure the view of an entire building before you. When we review a problem over and over again, it can get bigger and bigger in our eyes, crowding out even God. It is good to see a problem clear enough that we understand it, but at the same time we need to be turning it over to God and reminding ourselves how much bigger God is than our problem.

Elijah had accumulated a number of depression hits. He had a nutrition hit before eating the food the angel brought him, a social hit with his life being threatened and isolating himself, his circadian rhythm was off, he had a lifestyle hit by hiding in a cave away from sunlight, and a frontal lobe hit with negative thinking.

As opposed to getting into an argument with Elijah, God gave him an assignment to go anoint a couple of kings and a prophet who would eventually replace him. God also told him there were still 7,000 people in Israel who were not serving the false god, baal. Elijah did what God told him to do and as a result of that God was able to continue to use Elijah in wonderful ways, as well as the kings he anointed, and Elisha, the prophet who eventually replaced Elijah.

Like Moses in the wilderness and Jonah in the belly of a fish, it was in a quiet cave that Elijah was able to hear God. It is in quiet time with God, shutting out the rest of the world and listening, praying to God, reading the Bible, that we can hear His voice. Sometimes the best way to get out of the cave of depression is by sitting still and crying out to the Lord from that cave. God took Moses out of the wilderness to deliver people out of bondage, to lead them to the border of the Promised Land. God took Jonah out of the great fish to enter into ministry for Him. God took Elijah out of the cave and into the light. God will do the same for you.

Elijah's rehabilitation included good food, water, rest, exercise, getting him back to the Word of God, reminding him that he was not the only one in the world who had problems, and he was not the only person in the world whom God could use. God also reminded him that God was in charge, not him. The Lord demonstrated to Elijah that He was all powerful, but that God's powerful demonstrations were not as important in this case as hearing His still small voice. God put Elijah back to work with people who would be an encouragement and help to him, and to whom he could be of help. That is quite a list and a pretty good daily recipe for each of us.

Let me review this expansive and valuable list in bullet point fashion:

- Good food
- Water
- Rest
- Exercise
- The Bible
- Everyone has problems
- The world is not on our shoulders
- God is in charge
- God is all powerful
- God speaks to us by His still voice
- God is forgiving and merciful
- God-empowered obedience is more powerful than miracles

- Work is good

- Friendships are important

A big problem that many people face today is loneliness. We can still experience loneliness even if we live in large cities surrounded by people, or even if we use social media to connect with people from all over the globe. Not only can we still be lonely with social media and large communities, we might experience loneliness *because* of them. Being around people and connecting with people through an electronic device is not the same as face-to-face interaction or one-on-one communication.

When we are depressed, it is common for us not to want to be around other people. Like Elijah, we might want to isolate ourselves in a cave for forty days, but part of God's solution was sending Elijah out with a mission to be in contact with other people.

Once, before my wife Barbara and I met, she battled with depression. She found that part of her solution included getting involved with a local congregation, speaking with the minister and his wife, and getting involved in helping people who were in need. This gave her social interaction and gave her a purpose and a mission. It moved the focus off of herself to those whom she could be helping and placed her in a setting where she could be ministered to. As she ministered to others, she prayed for God to go before her and use her. As she saw the needs of others, it caused her to pray more than usual and to pray more for others than about her own needs. Thus, a cyclical process was taking place. She connected with God for help and ministering, then ministering to others caused her to connect even more closely with God. All of this was extremely healing for her.

Connecting and ministering to other people was part of what healed Barbara and Elijah of the depressions they were experiencing. In addition to that, being part of a local congregation and using our God-given gifts and talents in ministering to others will also help prevent depression.

Even before God drew Elijah out of the cave and sent him on a mission, He first spent time with Elijah. It might seem logical that being with other people is the solution to loneliness, but that is not the solution. We can have lots of friends and still be lonely. We can have no friends and not be lonely.

The real solution to loneliness is making a mental choice to be content with whatever is our current situation. Loneliness is more a state of mind than a lack of friends. God is always with us, thus in reality we are never really alone. While that is a reality, it takes faith to believe and accept that. If you don't have enough faith at the moment to believe that the God of the universe is right there with you, ask Him to give you more faith. He will give you more faith and He will give you the ability to believe and accept His promise of His presence with you. He loves you just as much as He loved Elijah.

Even though this earth is full of people, there may be times when there is no person who understands our situation or no one who cares about us. Sometimes that is reality and other times it just feels that way. Either way, God always cares and God always understands.

Even during those times when we are physically or emotionally isolated from any humans who care about us or who understand our situation, we can still be content and not lonely. Elijah was all alone, except for God, when he was by the Brook Cherith eating nothing but bread delivered by ravens for many months, if not years. Yet, there is no record of his being lonely or depressed at that time. Elijah chose to accept his situation and thus chose not to be lonely. He chose to be content.

Paul, who had years of isolation, wrote from prison:

> *Brothers and sisters, whatever is true, whatever is noble, whatever is right, whatever is pure, whatever is lovely, whatever is admirable—if anything is excellent or praiseworthy—think about such things. ...I have learned to be content whatever the circumstances. I know what it is to be in need, and I know what it is to have plenty. I have learned the secret of being content in any and every situation, whether well fed or hungry, whether living in plenty or in want. I can do all this through him who gives me strength* (Philippians 4:8,11-13 New International Version).

Regardless of your situation I encourage you to choose not to be lonely, to choose to be content, to choose to believe that God is with you and that He will give you the strength you need.

Some of the other things we recounted in God's prescription for Elijah included good food, fresh water, rest, exercise, and trusting in God. At Weimar Institute in Weimar, California, Dr. Nedley has developed a depression recovery program. In addition to that program, Weimar Institute has successfully helped people for more than forty years with a whole person healing lifestyle program that heals a wide range of aliments. The program is very simple and includes the prescription that God gave to Elijah. The program revolves around the acronym NEWSTART®. NEWSTART® stands for: N – healthy, balanced Nutrition, E – Exercise, W – fresh Water, S – right amount of Sunlight, T – Temperance (the right amounts of those things that are healthful and the total avoidance of those things that are harmful), A – fresh Air, R – proper Rest, T – Trust in God.

I will not take the space here to go into all the details of each of those topics, but notice that by following them properly we can eliminate many of the lifestyle hits that lead to depression. To learn more about the NEWSTART® program, you are encouraged to visit Weimar Institute's website or to go to the NEWSTART® Medical Clinic.

Barbara Gurien was working at a hospital in Jellico, Tennessee (on the Kentucky border), as an ultrasound technician when she became very depressed. Being Jewish and from New York City, she was experiencing culture shock living in the mountains in the deep south within the Bible Belt. She was lonely and was grieving not having a husband or children. As we have learned, those things in themselves are not enough hits to cause depression, but they were factors. For several months she didn't feel like eating, and she had a hard time sleeping. This of course just made matters worse by adding hits. Barbara couldn't figure out what was wrong, and she didn't even realize she was depressed.

One of the department heads at the hospital knew something was wrong and encouraged (pushed) her to go to Wildwood Lifestyle Center in Wildwood, Georgia. The Center operates a program based on the NEWSTART principles. Barbara was functioning on such a low level she could not even pack by herself. A friend of hers had to come over and help. In three weeks of following the program, Barbara's depression left, even though she still was not married, still did not have children, and was still in the deep South (this was in the 1980s).

Barbara was so happy with the results that she left her position in Jellico and took a position at the Wildwood Lifestyle Center. That was more than thirty years ago. She continues to follow the NEWSTART lifestyle principles.

Another aspect of Elijah's depression was his wish that God would just take his life; he wished that he was dead. In a sense, like Moses and Jonah, he was suicidal. If God had granted Elijah's prayer, or if Elijah had carried out his wish on his own, the people whom God had Elijah minister to would not have been reached through Elijah.

What I am going to write next might seem very shocking and I don't want it to be taken in a negative way. I understand that suicide is a very sensitive issue, but it needs to be addressed. I know that many people carry deep hurts in their hearts from their own attempted suicide or the suicide of someone they love. So please don't take these next words as a put-down of those who have attempted suicide or who have committed suicide. The purpose of this next observation is to help us realize what the door is that can allow us to contemplate and even do the unthinkable. When we are able and willing to see this trapdoor for what it is, we will better be able to avoid it.

Ready, here it comes: In a very real sense, in many cases, suicide is one of the most selfish acts a person can commit. The reality is that when we are tempted by the devil to commit suicide, we are only thinking of ourselves and not about how it will affect all those around us. He gets us thinking, "At least the pain will go away," "The troubles will all be gone," "I won't have to deal with it any-more," "I'm no good," "No one loves me or cares about me," etc. Self is the center of all of those thoughts. Yes, our pain might be gone, but what about the pain this action will inflict upon oth-ers. Yes, we will not have to deal with the troubles we are going through, but most likely someone else will have to pick up the pieces. A thought such as, "I can't do anything," is filled with pride. "I" is still the focus. It is not biblical humility to say, "I can't do any-thing," it is a satanic lie that focuses on ourselves and not what God can do and is doing in and through our lives.

When we are struggling with suicidal thoughts, the devil will also be telling us that no one else cares about us, but that is not reality; yet when we are in the midst of it and totally focused on ourselves, we are blinded to see all the care that people are show-ing toward us. And certainly God cares. When by God's grace we pull our eyes off of ourselves and think about how this will affect God and how it will affect others, we will better be able to turn away from the trapdoor.

Every time an early death takes place others are affected. We might not know who those people are. They may not even be part of our lives at the moment. They could be people who know peo-ple who would be affected by our death or people we would have met later on if we hadn't committed suicide. Everything has a rip-ple effect. God has a purpose for each one of us. The devil will deny that fact to us, and we may not know what that purpose is right now, but it is the truth—God has a purpose for you. You are spe-cial, you are important to Him. The only way to find out what that purpose is to its full extent, is to continue to live and let God play it out in our lives.

I was speaking with a person about someone we both knew who committed suicide. She stated he was in a better place. I asked her how she knew that. She said she just knew it. I said, "If that is the case, then let's all go. Let's all drink the Kool-Aid." Contrary to the 1989 movie, not all dogs go to heaven. It is very dangerous to think everyone automatically enters into some "better place" as soon as we die.

A young lady I know tried to commit suicide, a few times even. She ate a very good diet of a variety of fruits, grains, nuts, and vegetables, although sometimes it seemed that she did not eat enough. Some people even thought she was anorexic. Choosing to be thankful and choosing to see God's value in her were very helpful. In fact, many of the elements addressed in this book were helpful to her, including special intercessory prayer times that are discussed in Chapter 11.

After one of her suicide attempts she was very negative, stating over and over again she could not do anything, and everything was awful. When she would make a negative statement about herself, I told her she needed to tell me three positive things. She did not want to, but I threatened to end the conversation if she did not.

I gave her an assignment (which she begrudgingly agreed to), that each morning she would write to me one thing she was thankful for and one ability or trait or talent that God manifested in her. Every day she was to write: "I am thankful..." and "By God's grace I can..." To those who have not experienced such depression, this assignment might seem insignificant, but for some who have fallen into deep despair this assignment can be lifesaving.

At the beginning she did okay with the things to be thankful for, but it was a struggle and took prayer on her part and ours. As she did it each day, she started to far exceed the one thankful thought every day and started writing several things each day.

But the "God abilities" were very difficult for her to acknowledge. Finally she said she could boil water. I accepted that. The next day she said she could unboil water (by shutting off the stove). I accepted that also. Then she drew a blank and vehemently refused to acknowledge any positive thing God did in her.

This took much prayer and was a real spiritual struggle. Finally, upon her suggestion, she said if my wife and I told her things God manifested in her she would handwrite them 100 times. I don't necessarily suggest that everyone do that, but that was her suggestion. We started with some very simple but important and irrefutable things such as: by God's grace I can see; by God's grace I can eat; etc. Eventually, with much prayer on her part and ours, she was able to do this regularly and no longer needed our input.

Stinking thinking leads to a downward path, but an attitude of gratitude can greatly enhance our outlook and dramatically improve our attitude.

PAUSE, PONDER, AND PROCEED

1. If you have a tendency to be negative, I suggest you start a journal and each day write down at least one thing you are thankful for and at least one ability or character trait that God manifests through you. You

can do this for yourself, but it is also helpful to ask someone's permission to send it to them. This way you have someone to be accountable to, helping you to be consistent in this practice and giving you good, positive feedback.

2. In light of the many areas that Elijah struggled with and the variety of actions that God used to help him, I would like you to take a few minutes and consider the following questions:

    ▪ How can your diet or lifestyle be improved?

    ▪ Have you read from the Bible yet today? If not, I encourage you now to pause in this reading and pick up your Bible and read a section from it.

    ▪ Are you part of a local congregation? If not, begin praying that God leads you to the right one and then start looking for one.

    ▪ If you are part of a local congregation, are you involved in its mission? If you are not, how can you be? If you don't know, ask some of the leaders how you can get involved.

    ▪ What has God given you the ability to do, or what positive character trait does He manifest through you? If you answered "nothing" or "none," ask someone to answer it for you.

    ▪ What can you be thankful for today? (If you were able to read that question you definitely have some things you can be thankful for—even the ability to read.)

- Is your current problem bigger than God? If you answered "yes," read another passage out of the Bible.

- To whom are you currently ministering?

- Can you think of someone in this world who has more needs than you do? Or can you think of someone who has at least one need? How can you help them, or how can you help those who are helping them? (For example, by getting actively involved, offering a donation, praying for them, asking them how you can help, etc.)

AHAB—CONTROLLED BY OTHERS, DESIRING MORE

ELIJAH'S AND AHAB'S INTERACTIONS CONTINUED AFTER Elijah recovered from depression. In this chapter we look at King Ahab's bouts with depression. Most of this section is from the accounts in First Kings, chapter 21.

The Bible tells us, *"There was no one like Ahab who sold himself to do wickedness in the sight of the Lord,"* and then the Bible tells us why: *"because Jezebel his wife stirred him up"* (1 Kings 21:25).

Jezebel was the daughter of the king of the Sidonians. It might have been a truce marriage, but for whatever reason, they married. Ahab not only allowed Jezebel to worship her gods, but he chose to worship them as well and brought their worship into Israel.

We have already seen how vacillating Ahab was, shifting from being angry with Elijah to listening to Elijah, from trusting in the prophets of baal to trusting, to a small degree, in the God of Elijah, to letting Jezebel threaten Elijah with murder.

After all the things we read about in the previous chapter:

It came to pass after these things that Naboth the Jezreelite had a vineyard which was in Jezreel, next to the palace of Ahab king of Samaria. So Ahab spoke to Naboth, saying, "Give me your vineyard, that I may have it for a vegetable garden, because it is near, next to my house; and for it I will give you a vineyard better than it. Or, if it seems good to you, I will give you its worth in money."

But Naboth said to Ahab, "The Lord forbid that I should give the inheritance of my fathers to you!"

So Ahab went into his house sullen and displeased because of the word which Naboth the Jezreelite had spoken to him; for he had said, "I will not give you the inheritance of my fathers." And he lay down on his bed, and turned away his face, and would eat no food. But Jezebel his wife came to him, and said to him, "Why is your spirit so sullen that you eat no food?"

He said to her, "Because I spoke to Naboth the Jezreelite, and said to him, 'Give me your vineyard for money; or else, if it pleases you, I will give you another vineyard for it.' And he answered, 'I will not give you my vineyard.'"

Then Jezebel his wife said to him, "You now exercise authority over Israel! Arise, eat food, and let your heart be cheerful; I will give you the vineyard of Naboth the Jezreelite" (1 Kings 21:1-7).

Jezebel wrote letters in Ahab's name, sealed them with his seal, and sent the letters to the elders and the nobles and had them murder Naboth. When Jezebel heard that Naboth had been stoned and was dead, she said to Ahab, *"Arise, take possession of the vineyard of Naboth the Jezreelite, which he refused to give you for money; for Naboth is not alive, but dead"* (1 Kings 21:15). Ahab got up and went down to take possession of the vineyard of Naboth.

> *Then the word of the Lord came to Elijah the Tishbite, saying, "Arise, go down to meet Ahab king of Israel, who lives in Samaria. There he is, in the vineyard of Naboth, where he has gone down to take possession of it. You shall speak to him, saying, 'Thus says the Lord: "Have you murdered and also taken possession?"' And you shall speak to him, saying, 'Thus says the Lord: "In the place where dogs licked the blood of Naboth, dogs shall lick your blood, even yours."'"*
>
> *So Ahab said to Elijah, "Have you found me, O my enemy?"*
>
> *And he answered, "I have found you, because you have sold yourself to do evil in the sight of the Lord: 'Behold, I will bring calamity on you. I will take away your posterity, and will cut off from Ahab every male in Israel, both bond and free. I will make your house like the house of Jeroboam the son of Nebat, and like the house of Baasha the son of Ahijah, because of the provocation with which you have provoked Me to anger, and made Israel sin.'*

And concerning Jezebel the Lord also spoke, saying, 'The dogs shall eat Jezebel by the wall of Jezreel.' The dogs shall eat whoever belongs to Ahab and dies in the city, and the birds of the air shall eat whoever dies in the field" (1 Kings 21:17-24).

All those events took place just as God prophesied through Elijah, but you can read those exciting parts of Ahab's story in your own Bible. Wouldn't you like it if every time some drek (Yiddish word you don't need to know the meaning of) like Ahab did some dirty deed that God would immediately send an Elijah to rebuke him and tell him he's gonna get it? But that is not always how God works. He prefers to use His still, small voice.

It really took guts on Elijah's part to meet Ahab in that vineyard. That is true meekness—humble before God, bold (when necessary) before people. Why did God send Elijah? Was it just so Elijah could let Ahab have it and give him the tongue-lashing he deserved? No, it was because God loved Ahab. Yes, God loved Ahab, even that vacillating, cry-baby thief, Ahab. God was sending a wake-up warning to Ahab through Elijah.

"So it was, when Ahab heard those words, that he tore his clothes and put sackcloth on his body, and fasted and lay in sackcloth, and went about mourning" (1 Kings 21:27). That sounds more like repentance than depression, and the next words in the Bible confirm it: *"And the word of the Lord came to Elijah, saying, 'See how Ahab has humbled himself before Me? Because he humbled himself before Me, I will not bring the calamity in his days. In the days of his son I will bring the calamity on his house"* (1 Kings 21:28-29). Oh what a merciful God we serve who even had mercy on one such as

Ahab of whom it is written, *"There was no one like Ahab who sold himself to do wickedness in the sight of the Lord."*

How much more will He be merciful to you and me, no matter how wicked we have been, if we repent. If God can be so merciful with us and with the Ahabs of this world, can't He give us that same mercy toward the Ahabs in our lives? Yes, He can.

Ahab had become sullen and depressed when he did not get what he wanted, Naboth's vineyard. Even though Ahab had more than most people, he wanted more. He did not necessarily want all the land, just the land next to his. Of course with that logic, when the land next to his became his, the one next to that became the land next to his, and something to be desired. Thus it would become a never-ending process until all the world was his. Greed and discontentment are never satisfied with more.

Contentment is not based on what we have; it is based on a choice we make. We do not "become" content, we "choose" to be content. Paul wrote from a dungeon where he had been unjustly imprisoned:

> *I am not saying this because I am in need—for whatever circumstance I am in, I have learned to be content. I know what it is to live with humble means, and I know what it is to live in prosperity. In any and every circumstance I have learned the secret of contentment—both to be filled and to go hungry, to have abundance and to suffer need. I can do all things through Messiah who strengthens me* (Philippians 4:11-13 TLV).

Hopefully you and I are not falsely accused and locked in a dungeon right now, but even if we are, through Messiah we can choose to be content in whatever state we are currently in.

In the fabulous allegorical book *The Pilgrim's Progress,* the main character and his friend Hopeful become discontent with the path God laid out for them and they went off the straight and narrow path toward heaven in search of an easier, more pleasant path. They begin to follow a man named Vain-Confidence, who ends up falling into a pit. The pilgrims begin to chide themselves for their wrong choices as a torrential rain pours upon them and a flood of water begins to rise, impeding their way back. They eventually find a little shelter and fall asleep. In the morning Giant Despair, the owner of the land, finds them and takes them to Doubting Castle where he locks them up. Giant Despair beats them mercilessly and encourages them to take their own lives, which they strongly consider.

Hopeful encourages his companion with these words,

> Indeed our present condition is dreadful, and death would be far more welcome to me than thus for ever to abide; but yet let us consider, the Lord of the country to which we are going hath said, "Thou shalt do no murder," no, not to another man's person. Much more, then, are we forbidden to take his counsel to kill ourselves. Besides, he that kills another can but commit murder upon his body; but for one to kill himself, is to kill body and soul at once. And, moreover, my brother, thou talkest of ease in the grave; but hast thou forgotten that "no murderer hath eternal life." Let us consider again, that

all the law is not in the hand of Giant Despair; others, so far as I can understand, have been taken by him as well as we, and yet have escaped out of his hand: who knows but that God who made the world may cause that Giant Despair may die that, at some time or other, he may forget to lock us in?—or, but he may in a short time have another of his fits before us, and may lose the use of his limbs? And if ever that should come to pass again, for my part I am resolved to pluck up the heart of a man, and to try my utmost to get from under his hand. I was a fool that I did not try to do it before; but however, my brother, let us be patient, and endure awhile; the time may come that may give us a happy release; but let us not be our own murderers.

After a few more beatings and again contemplating suicide, they remember to pray. As they pray they remember they have with them the Key of Promise that can open any door. They use it and escape the dungeon.

If we are discontent with the path God has laid out for us, or with our current situation, we also have the power of prayer and the Key of Promise. We have already read one such promise: "I can do all things through Messiah who strengthens me." Yes, we can choose to be content whatever our lot or circumstances. There are many wonderful promises in the Bible that are the keys to set us free from doubt and despair.

If, like the pilgrims, we are being beaten by Giant Despair because of our self-loathing over our wrong choices, then we have another wonderful promise: *"If we confess our sins, He is faithful*

*and just to forgive us of all our sins and cleanse us from all unrigh-
teousness"* (1 John 1:9).

Another problem Ahab had was that he allowed himself to be
controlled by his wife Jezebel. Even though he was king, he was
insecure about who he was and so he allowed other people and
circumstances to control his actions and his feelings. No one else
should control us. We are subject to God and God alone. We can
listen to other people's opinions, we can heed their advice, but we
should not blindly follow or be controlled by anyone.

We can be secure in who we are because of God's great love
for us. Our worth is not in ourselves or our abilities but in the
price that was paid for us—the sacrifice of the Messiah Himself.
We are princes and princesses of God because He has adopted us
as His children. We are co-inheritors with Him and beloved in
Him. Since we have surrendered our lives to the God of heaven and
become His servants and children, we no longer need to fear anyone or be controlled by anyone.

PAUSE, PONDER, AND PROCEED

1. If you are stuck in Doubting Castle or are being
   beaten by Giant Despair, resolve, by God's grace, to
   pluck up your heart, and try your utmost, by God's
   power, to get out from under Giant Despair's hand.

2. If you have been following Vain-Confidence, or have
   been self-loathing over mistakes you made, choose
   to change course. Accept the Messiah's forgiveness
   because of His death on your behalf for your sins;
   and be confident of this one thing, that He who has

begun a good work in you will bring it to completion (see Philippians 1:6).

3. If you are allowing yourself to be controlled by others, ask God to give you the courage to mentally break from their control and to be led only by God. Pray this every time you sense you are allowing yourself to be controlled by others.

4. If you are discontent over your circumstances or perceived lacking, take a moment now and give it all to God and let Him work His wonderful promises in you, giving you contentment and victory.

Naomi—Bitter Grief

Naomi was so depressed by her situation she wanted to have people call her bitter. She felt like her life was nothing but bitterness. Up to that point she had experienced a lot of bitter experiences that most people would find depressing.

About 300 or so years after Moses, during the time of the Judges, before there was a king in Israel, there was a famine in Naomi's homeland of Bethlehem, Israel. Due to the famine, her family moved to Moab. Naomi's husband died there. Her sons married Moabite women, which at first must have been a disappointment since God tells us not to be unequally yoked with those not of our faith. Then both her sons died. She really was left with nothing. No family, in a foreign land, with no one to take care of her in her old age. She had nothing to give her hope in the present or in the future. After ten years in Moab, Naomi decided to travel back to Bethlehem.

So, what were Naomi's depression hits that we know of? Terrible grief due to the loss of husband and both children. It has been said there is no grief like the loss of a child, maybe because it seems so unnatural. Parents are not supposed to outlive their children. We have a word for people who lose a spouse; we call them a widow or a widower. We have a word for people who lose their parents; we call them orphans. But we do not have a word to describe people who lose their children. It is as if we can't even talk about it or name it because it is so grievous.

Naomi had the stress of moving, and almost no social network, plus she had no hope. Naomi was experiencing a social hit from the loss of loved ones, possibly a circadian rhythm hit if she was not sleeping well. Possibly a lifestyle hit if she had not been exercising and getting out in the sun and fresh air.

Naomi might have had a frontal lobe hit if she was not using her brain for abstract thinking and if she was feeling guilty for leaving Israel, moving to Moab, letting her sons marry Moabite women, and staying in Moab so long. She also felt abandoned by God saying, *"...the hand of the Lord has gone out against me!" "...the Almighty has dealt very bitterly with me. ...the Lord has testified against me, and the Almighty has afflicted me."* (Ruth 1:13, 20-21).

When Naomi decided to go back to Israel, her daughters-in-law initially started to go with her, but she encouraged them to return to their families. At first neither wanted to leave her. Orpah finally did, but Ruth stayed with her and said these memorable lines, *"Entreat me not to leave you, or to turn back from following after you; for wherever you will go, I will go; and wherever you lodge, I will lodge; your people shall be my people, your God, my God. Where you die, I will die, and there will I be buried. The Lord do so to me, and more also, if anything but death parts you and me"* (Ruth 1:16-17).

Although Naomi did not realize or fully appreciate it at the time, Ruth's commitment was a lifesaver for Naomi.

Right after Ruth proclaimed that amazing commitment to Naomi, the Bible says that when Naomi saw that Ruth was determined to go with her, she *"stopped speaking to her"* (Ruth 1:18). Yes, it might mean she just stopped entreating her to stay in Moab, but Naomi might have stopped speaking to Ruth because she might have been initially upset with Ruth for staying with her. Naomi thought it was her responsibility to provide for Ruth, indicated by Naomi saying, *"Are there still sons in my womb, that they may be your husbands?"* (Ruth 1:11). Thus, she might have looked at Ruth's staying with her as adding to the burdens she was already carrying. Even when there are some people around us trying to help us, we might see them as more of a problem than a help. A friend might want to visit to cheer us up or keep us company, and we may look at it as a burden upon us to entertain them.

Naomi might have stopped speaking to Ruth at that point because she was upset with Ruth for not leaving her alone. At this point Naomi might have wanted to crawl in a ball and be left alone. But Ruth would not let that happen. The Bible does not record Ruth saying anything more at that point either. She may have kept quiet and just remained by Naomi's side. Sometimes that is the best thing we can do. Sometimes it is not words, but just our presence that is needed—even when it is not wanted.

Naomi saw no hope in her future, and she rejected or did not acknowledge the people who were there to help her. It is one of the strange conundrums we experience when we are depressed. Sometimes when we are depressed we complain no one is there for us while at the same time we push away the very ones who are trying to help us. Is there anyone you are consciously or unconsciously shutting out of your life right now?

I was visiting with a person who had recently attempted suicide. He was lamenting there was no one to help him. I pointed out I was listening to him. (What was I...chopped liver?) He was forced to acknowledge my presence. I pointed out some of the ways his wife was trying to help him. He admitted she was a tremendous help. Without my pointing these things out, he did not see them for himself. Are there people in your life who are there for you, but you are forgetting to acknowledge them?

When Naomi and Ruth reached Bethlehem, the people were happy to see Naomi but she was depressed and told them to call her Marah, the Hebrew word for bitter. To make a great story short, Ruth found a job gleaning in the fields. It just happened to be the field of a near kinsman named Boaz who ended up marrying Ruth. He provided for both Ruth and Naomi, and fathered a grandchild for Naomi named Obed. Obed became the grandfather of King David, the ancestor of the Messiah. I encourage you to read the entire account yourself in the Bible book titled Ruth.

Naomi suddenly snapped out of her depression after she found out that the field Ruth was gleaning in was owned by Boaz. Now Naomi had hope. Hope made all the difference.

Naomi experienced tremendous heartache and grief. You might be experiencing tremendous heartache and grief right now, maybe the bitterest experience of your life. There is a wonderful Bible promise that *"all things work together for good to those who love God, to those who are the called according to His purpose"* (Romans 8:28).

If Ruth's husband (one of Naomi's sons) had not died, Ruth never would have married Boaz, David would never have been born, and it would have changed everything regarding how the Messiah would come to this world. God has a purpose even in death, even if we don't see it for several generations. God turned Naomi's horrible experiences into the very things that brought about King David and the Messiah. Maybe "God only knows" what good He is going to bring out of the horrible experience you are going through, but His promise is just as much for you as it was for Naomi. Trust in His promises.

There is no guarantee God is going to raise our dead loved ones from the grave so we will see them again in this life. God did not raise up Naomi's husband or her two sons for her. But we do have an assurance that if our loved ones accepted the Messiah's sacrifice for us, and became filled with the Holy Spirit and God's love, they will be resurrected to everlasting life. If we do the same, we will see them and be with them again for eternity. If they rejected God's love—and none of us will be fully sure of that until the judgment of God is revealed—this certainly is a harder grief to bear, but we still know God loved them and He had given them the gift of free choice.

There is no guarantee God will give us another spouse or more children. He did not do that for Naomi. Not that having another spouse or more children would ever replace the ones who have passed away. After we experience the death of a loved one, whether or not we ever receive another spouse or more children, we enter into the next stage of our lives.

There is no guarantee we will have a wonderful daughter-in-law like Ruth, or a wonderful earthly near relative like Boaz who will provide a wonderful grandchild and financial stability. But we do have a wonderful near Relative in the Messiah and He has promised to *"never leave you nor forsake you"* (Deuteronomy 31:6). He has promised to *"supply all your need according to His riches in glory..."* (Philippians 4:19). All our need includes our social needs for friends and loved ones. Our emotional needs for comfort, strength, and a sound mind. Our financial need—the key word is need. And our physical need—again the key word is need.

Naomi could see no hope for her future. You might not be seeing any hope for your future. You may feel the same. But there is a marvelous line in a book titled *Desire of the Ages* that says, "Our heavenly Father has a thousand ways to provide for us, of which we know nothing. Those who accept the one principle of making the service and honor of God supreme will find perplexities vanish, and a plain path before their feet."[1] Even if you cannot think of a solution to your situation, God can think of one thousand, all of which are good for you.

PAUSE, PONDER, AND PROCEED

1. Are you currently grieving the loss of a loved one? Several people in this book experienced that type of grief, thus we will be discussing ways to cope with it in various chapters. This will especially be done

in the chapter entitled "Martha and Mary, Stages of Grief." Feel free to jump ahead to that chapter if this is an area you are specifically dealing with at this time.

2. Have you been unconsciously pushing people away who, out of love, have been trying to support you?

3. Use this as your time in the wilderness, belly-of-the fish private time, to cry out to God and to listen to His response from His Word. At the same time write a note to those whom you have pushed away, letting them know you appreciate them. Try to explain to them your desire for space.

4. If you are able to admit your need for company, even if you don't feel like it, invite them to visit you. If you don't feel like talking, let them know that and that you just want their quiet company.

5. If you are not ready for a visit, give them a time when they should check back with you. The time you set will vary depending upon whom you are writing to, but it should be in the not-too-distant future, maybe a day or so. Certainly we should not go more than a week without at least someone having our permission to check on us, especially if we are struggling with grief or depression.

6. If you have been through some bitter experiences in your past and see no hope for your future, ask God to give you faith to believe these words and say them out loud, "All things will work together for good to

me because I love God, and am called according to His purpose. God will provide for my needs according to His riches in glory."

NOTE

1. Ellen G. White, *Desire of the Ages* (Nampa, ID: Pacific Press Publishing Assoc., 2002), 330.

8

DAVID—NEGLECTED AND REJECTED

DAVID WAS A PERSON OF WHOM WE HAVE ENOUGH INFORMA-
tion about to identify some developmental hits. David seems to
have been a neglected or under-wanted child. You might be sur-
prised at that, so let's look at what the Bible says.

When the prophet Samuel came to visit David's father, Jesse,
he invited the household to come to a sacrifice. Jesse brought seven
of his sons but left David in the fields with the sheep. How would
that make you feel? Now maybe there was no one else in all of
Bethlehem who could have watched the sheep that night; but nevertheless, being the only one not at the sacrifice must have been
keenly felt by David. Whether the slights against us are real or

imaginary, they still hurt the same and still have the same effects on us emotionally.

Later, when his brothers were on the front lines of a war with the Philistines and Goliath, Jesse sent David with some food for his brothers (I guess this time they were able to find a "keeper" for the sheep). Instead of being grateful he brought them some home-cooked food, they said, *"Why did you come down here? And with whom have you left those few sheep in the wilderness? I know your pride and the insolence of your heart, for you have come down to see the battle"* (1 Samuel 17:28). His brothers' reaction to this messenger with food could reveal much about how he was treated in the home.

Looking at David's early life we can see several possible hits. David was left out in the field by his father when the prophet came to their home, and he was berated by his older brothers. That sounds like a social hit. Later he was rejected and hunted by his king/father-in-law and had to hide in the wilderness. During that time it is very likely David had a hard time getting a balanced food diet, even having to beg for food, thus he could have experienced a nutrition hit. He might have also had a genetic hit as we read how his great-grandmother Naomi had a bout with depression.

David's other problems included his son raping his daughter, one son killing another son, and a son overthrowing his kingdom and then hunting him down to kill him. Later another son proclaimed himself king while David was still alive. And we think we have problems? David's life from beginning to end was filled with major life-threatening and life-altering problems.

David's key to sanity was talking out his problems with God, then trusting and praising God. Look at some of these songs he wrote:

> *I am weary with my groaning; all night I make my bed swim; I drench my couch with my tears. My eye wastes away because of grief; it grows old because of all my enemies. Depart from me, all you workers of iniquity; for the Lord has heard the voice of my weeping. The Lord has heard my supplication; the Lord will receive my prayer* (Psalm 6:6-9).

All night David was groaning and crying (can you relate?) because he had real enemies trying to take his life, but he chose to trust that God heard him and was going to help him.

> *All day they twist my words; all their thoughts are against me for evil.* [Does that sound familiar to you? But David didn't stop there.] *They gather together, they hide, they mark my steps, when they lie in wait for my life. Shall they escape by iniquity? In anger cast down the peoples, O God! You number my wanderings; put my tears into Your bottle; are they not in Your book? When I cry out to You, then my enemies will turn back; this I know, because God is for me. In God (I will praise His word), in the Lord (I will praise His word), in God I have put my trust; I will not be afraid. What can man do to me?* (Psalm 56:5-11)

David didn't deny his problems, nor did he try to forget them or drown them out with alcohol, drugs, or busyness. He spoke with God and left them there, trusting that God was bigger than his problems.

In Psalm 40 David mentions God hearing his cry and bringing him up out of a horrible pit. I doubt David was in a physical pit; this sounds more like a pit of depression. David lamented that innumerable evils surrounded him. He confessed that his sins were more than the hairs of his head and had overtaken him so much that he could not look up and his heart failed him. David acknowledged that he was poor and needy as he called out to God not to delay His help and deliverance.

Throughout this song/poem/psalm, David mixed words of hope and faith along with the realities of his cries, external enemies, fear-induced panic attack causing his heart to fail, and guilt. Even with those realities David said:

> *I waited patiently for the Lord; and He inclined to me....*
> *He...set my feet upon a rock, and established my steps. He*
> *has put a new song in my mouth—Praise to our God; ...*
> *and will trust in the Lord. ...Many, O Lord my God, are*
> *Your wonderful works which You have done; and Your*
> *thoughts toward us cannot be recounted to You in order;*
> *if I would declare and speak of them, they are more*
> *than can be numbered. ...I delight to do Your will, O*
> *my God, and Your law is within my heart. ..."The Lord*
> *be magnified!" ...Yet the Lord thinks upon me* (Psalm
> 40:1-5,8,16-17).

Stark realities of the problems we face do not cancel out having faith and hope. Also, true hope does not ignore the reality of problems. We do face real problems, but at the same time we have God who is bigger than all our problems, who loves us supremely. That is as truthful a reality as any difficulty we face.

Music was a big part of David's life and no doubt helped him cope with the very real and huge problems he had to deal with in his life. We will see in the chapter about King Saul how David's harp helped King Saul cope with his anxieties.

One of the times we see the magnanimity of David was when King Saul was chasing David through the wilderness with an army of 3,000 men to kill David. David and his few men were hiding in a cave near Ein Gedi, in the desert near the Dead Sea. Saul decided to take a nap, and out of all the thousands of caves in that area he "happened" to end up in David's cave. David's men suggested that this was of the Lord and that David should kill Saul. David refused, stating that it was not for him to take the life of the Lord's anointed. David did sneak up next to King Saul and cut the corner of his garment. When Saul awoke and left the cave David shouted out to him, showing him the evidence of Saul's vulnerability and demonstrating that he had no animosity toward the king. Saul relented for a time from stalking David. He invited David to come back with him, but David did not.

Actually, David did a similar thing at another time. That time David took the water jug and spear that were near the king.

David forgave, without retaliating, even though he had the opportunity to, and most likely would have been considered justified in doing so. Yet at the same time he did not foolishly go back with the king. Forgiveness does not forget. It is not stupid. It is not codependent. It does not excuse or wipe away wrongs. It faces them for what they are, but at the same time chooses not to hold on to anger and revenge. Forgiveness seeks justice, yes. But revenge, never.

Too often people have gone back into abusive situations, being self-deceived that they are being forgiving. That is not forgiveness in the biblical sense of the word. Forgiveness forgives, but it does not necessarily open itself up to be hurt again.

Even with God's forgiveness toward us, a price has to be paid, both the Messiah's death as our substitute, and our death to self as well. As Moses wrote, *"The Lord your God will circumcise your heart"* (Deuteronomy 30:6). Similarly Ezekiel wrote:

> *Repent, and turn from all your transgressions, so that iniquity will not be your ruin. Cast away from you all the transgressions which you have committed, and get yourselves a new heart and a new spirit.... I will give you a new heart and put a new spirit within you; I will take the heart of stone out of your flesh and give you a heart of flesh. I will put My Spirit within you and cause you to walk in My statutes, and you will keep My judgments and do them. Then you shall dwell in the land that I gave to your fathers; you shall be My people, and I will be your God* (Ezekiel 18:30-31; 36:26-28).

In order for us to receive forgiveness from God, we have to "pay" for it with our old heart, our carnal desires, our inclinations to do wrong, our bad habits. How do we make that payment? Simply by confessing those desires, inclinations, habits, and sins. We turn them over to God with confession. God transfers them to His Son who puts them into Himself and who killed them when He died. He took the punishment we deserve by taking the sins we have, and He gives us the righteousness He has. God *"made Him who knew no sin to be sin for us, that we might become the righteousness of God in Him"* (2 Corinthians 5:21).

You are *"a new creation; old things have passed away; behold, all things have become new"* (2 Corinthians 5:17). It is better than putting garbage in your garbage can at night and the sanitation department taking it and giving you gold in its place. It is a pretty good deal, and it is that simple.

While God can immediately give us forgiveness toward someone who hurt us, we must be careful not to extend trust until a new heart and new life is seen lived out consistently for a long period of time. For major offenses we might want to wait to extend trust until we see consistent changes in their lives. It might be safe to wait at least a year, give or take. With some offenses, we might want to wait to see a consistent change lived out longer; for other offenses we must never extend trust. Forgiveness, yes, unconditionally and always—but trust is conditional. Forgiveness releases us of the anger, but it does not necessarily release them of the consequences.

Even when David was at one of the lowest points of his life, when he was hunted by King Saul and living in a cave, he wrote Psalm 57, which says:

> *Be merciful to me, O God, be merciful to me! For my soul trusts in You; and in the shadow of Your wings I will make my refuge, until these calamities have passed by. I will cry out to God Most High, to God who performs all things for me. He shall send from heaven and save me; He reproaches the one who would swallow me up. God shall send forth His mercy and His truth. My soul is*

among lions; I lie among the sons of men who are set on fire, whose teeth are spears and arrows, and their tongue a sharp sword.

Be exalted, O God, above the heavens; let Your glory be above all the earth. They have prepared a net for my steps; my soul is bowed down; they have dug a pit before me; into the midst of it they themselves have fallen. My heart is steadfast, O God, my heart is steadfast; I will sing and give praise. Awake, my glory! Awake, lute and harp! I will awaken the dawn. I will praise You, O Lord, among the peoples; I will sing to You among the nations. For Your mercy reaches unto the heavens, and Your truth unto the clouds. Be exalted, O God, above the heavens; let Your glory be above all the earth.

God spoke to Moses in the wilderness on a mountain, He reached Jonah inside a giant fish, Elijah in a cave, and here we see David praising God while being hunted for his life while hiding in a cave. We are seeing a pattern of the importance of alone time with God. Depression can feel like being alone in a cave, but when we invite God into that cave it becomes illuminated and we can see the path out to the light.

Another great experience we see in David's life that kept him from falling into depression was his willingness to receive rebuke, accept responsibility for mistakes, confess his faults, repent, and receive forgiveness.

David had really blown it. He had committed adultery with Uriah's wife. Then to cover up her pregnancy he brought Uriah home from the war and then sent him back to the front lines to be killed. After Uriah's death David married Uriah's wife Bathsheba. God's prophet Nathan came to David and told David a parable to bring conviction to him. Nathan told David that a rich man with lots of animals took the only lamb of a poor man and served it to his guest. David, being a shepherd at heart, was enraged and said that man should be punished. Nathan told David that he was "the man" whose sin against Uriah was seen by God. David could have had Nathan killed; instead, he took the rebuke and repented of his sin.

Like unforgiveness, a guilty conscience will eat away at us and make us susceptible to depression.

It was after that experience that David wrote Psalm 51. If you have a guilty conscience because of some sin you have participated in, I invite you to pray David's prayer from Psalm 51 and receive God's forgiveness and cleansing:

Have mercy upon me, O God, according to Your loving-kindness; according to the multitude of Your tender mercies, blot out my transgressions. Wash me thoroughly from my iniquity, and cleanse me from my sin. For I acknowledge my transgressions, and my sin is always before me. Against You, You only, have I sinned, and done this evil in Your sight— that You may be found just when You speak, and blameless when You judge.

Behold, I was brought forth in iniquity, and in sin my mother conceived me. Behold, You desire truth in the inward parts, and in the hidden part You will make me to know wisdom. Purge me with hyssop, and I shall be clean; wash me, and I shall be whiter than snow.

Make me hear joy and gladness, that the bones You have broken may rejoice. Hide Your face from my sins, and blot out all my iniquities. Create in me a clean heart, O God, and renew a steadfast spirit within me. Do not cast me away from Your presence, and do not take Your Holy Spirit from me.

Restore to me the joy of Your salvation, and uphold me by Your generous Spirit. Then I will teach transgressors Your ways, and sinners shall be converted to You. Deliver me from the guilt of bloodshed, O God, the God of my salvation, and my tongue shall sing aloud of Your righteousness. O Lord, open my lips, and my mouth shall show forth Your praise. For You do not desire sacrifice, or else I would give it; You do not delight in burnt offering. The sacrifices of God are a broken spirit, a broken and a contrite heart—these, O God, You will not despise....

Juanita Kretchmar's nervous system was in shambles. For several years she suffered from depression. A doctor stated that within two months she would need to be institutionalized because he felt she was headed for a complete nervous breakdown. He said her condition was irreversible. She felt hopeless and feared losing her sanity.

Even though she was a godly woman who had grown up in a godly home and was married to a godly man and was raising her children to be godly people, the doctor's statement reverberated in her mind so much that she withdrew from attending religious services and would not leave her home. She popped a thermometer in her mouth frequently—hoping for a treatable, physical ailment to resolve her despair. No one knew her troubled thoughts. Sometime before this low time in her life hit her, Juanita had stopped having a personal devotional time, with daily reading and prayer.

Days passed and restful sleep would not come. She impulsively pulled a book off a bookshelf in their home and she read how the author, Ellen White, experienced a time when her nervous energy was depleted but she started praying every five minutes and she became restored. It had been days since Juanita had left the house, being fearful of being in a public place when the doctor's verdict might suddenly come true. But because of what she had just read, Juanita cautiously accepted her husband's invitation to go for a ride in the car. She kept her head down, watching the hands on her watch. She prayed silently for God to keep her sane for just five minutes. After five minutes she prayed again for sanity for five more minutes. She continued this way every five minutes through-out that day.

A friend mentioned how a Bible promise had helped her: *"He gives power to the faint; and to them that have no might He increases strength"* (Isaiah 40:29). Juanita felt like God was speaking directly to her. Hope took over. With a change in attitude, and with prayer every few minutes, slowly her strength returned. The ability to sleep returned as well. By God's grace, instead of confinement at the end of the two-month period, she had resumed all her earlier home and congregational responsibilities.[1]

Juanita went on to run a ministry with more than 25 employees and had a yearly budget in the millions (in the 1990s). Now in her 80s, Juanita is still active for the Lord. She is leading a congregation and is the director of a Bible-based radio station, WHNJ, in the Florida Keys. She also directs a free blood-pressure and health-screening van ministry.

Here is a story to illustrate how different her whole life has gone from being depressed and self-absorbed to only being other-people focused. I have known Juanita personally for more than thirty years and I will testify that this story is exactly how she lives her life by God's grace. In Juanita's words:

I found myself, around midnight, riding in the back of an ambulance careening through the streets of Miami, trying to have a sense of sanity as I lay there staring at the clock on the wall at one end of the ambulance and wondering quietly how on earth I'd managed to get myself in such a situation. Suddenly, a quiet question came to my mind, "Who are you?" I responded inwardly to the question. I said my name and how I pray for people who call or write or ask for prayer in some way. Then came a second question that stopped me, "What are you doing here?"

What was I doing there? Riding in the back of an ambulance (for the first time in my life) in the middle of the night somewhere in Miami? My thoughts reviewed the previous hours quickly...The day had been a blur since after our staff worship. We had knelt for closing prayer at about 10:15 that morning. I recalled that during the prayer I'd started to feel really ill. Strange for me...feeling just awful. I had not arisen from my knees. I couldn't. Lynn, gathering her belongings after worship, saw me still on the floor and asked, "Are you OK?"

I looked at her and said honestly, "NO!"

No one was used to that kind of answer out of my mouth, but they knew I sometimes stay longer in prayer, so she let me know before she left my house that I should call her if I needed something.

I was in bad shape. Unexplainable and indefinable to me! I didn't begin feeling better right away as I expected I would. I crawled up onto the couch and lay down. A sequence of events in the hours following included intervention on the phone with pleas from competent, skilled (but frustrated with me) medical caregiver family members who lived in other states. But their loving urging, punctuated with the mobilization of Lynn and Brad, refused to accept my stubborn "NO" answers about going anywhere. Hours later I lay on that gurney wondering how I could have gotten myself into such a predicament—wasting everyone's time and lots of money. I'd already been to one hospital that was sending me to another where they said facilities were equipped for surgery their tests had shown needed to be done, quickly!

But the question begged an answer from me, "WHAT was I doing there?" However my own answer to the first question about "who are you?" began clearing up the bewilderment in my mind as to what was going on. As I began recalling how...God longs for every person to know how MUCH He loves them, longs to have everyone know He wants each to have the place reserved in heaven for them...how anyone and everyone can be in His kingdom, if they will choose to accept the invitation. And how He wants us to share that invitation everywhere!

Suddenly it hit me; I may even have said the words aloud to God as we neared our Miami destination: "So that is what this is all about! You probably have some medical caregivers up in that hospital in Miami whom You want told about how much You love them...You need someone to tell them, don't You?...And it's urgent, isn't it?"

I looked upward and I don't know if I lifted my hand outwardly—but I did inwardly—as I responded, "I'm Your 'girl'...I want to be the one whom You are looking for! That's why You have me going up here! Someone up here needs to hear of Yeshua's love and very personal plan for each of us. Only the Messiah knew the depth of His Father's love, and made that huge sacrifice for us! You are so amazing...You have such a plan for all our lives! I'm going to pray with them and tell them about Your love—Your personal plan for them! Yes, I am! I felt almost giddy with excitement. I was on an assignment from God!

I would need to leave each one with some literature. Radio station WHNJ's business cards would be perfect!

It turned out to be some two dozen persons with whom I got to pray during the next three days in my hospital room-turned-chapel. It was such a privilege God let me be there. Hospital staff opened up about their prayer burdens as we prayed together. The very last woman fell on my neck, weeping, as she shared the personal abandonment she had just experienced. I showed her Jeremiah 29:11. She read it, "I know the thoughts that I think toward you, says the Lord, thoughts of peace and not of evil, to give you a future and a hope." It was like a personal message to her from God. Her shoulders straightened. Her eyes that had been filled with tears now glistened with hope. I knew if it had been for no one else, for her I had been sent there! And, no, surgery wasn't wise at that time during that pancreatitis emergency. (I did have a sick gall bladder removed the following month.)

Now one other notable thing about that Miami hospital "assignment." Within minutes of God's revelation of "what" that emergency trip was all about, the "indescribable sick" feelings I had had totally lifted! Other than the reports from lab work, etc., many caregivers told me, "You don't look sick" or "You surely look well to me." (But God had to keep me there until all His "caregiver-patients" He needed to have told of His personal love and plan for their lives had heard).[2]

It would certainly have been acceptable and logical for Juanita to be totally concerned for her own health and well-being under the circumstances of being medically diagnosed with an emergency pancreatitis attack. But Juanita has chosen to put God and others before herself. (I have seen it over and over again during the past thirty years of knowing her.) It is real. One of the ways Juanita keeps from falling back into a depressed state is by continually surrendering to God's will and being willing to be used by Him at all times.

Would you like to be able to have peace in your mind and heart, and the security of knowing you are on a mission for God, even if you are in a life-threatening emergency? Or simply in your ordinary, mundane days? Well, God's peace and purpose is available to each of us just as it has been for Juanita. It starts with knowing and believing that you are God's child and that He has a plan for each day of your life to be His noble representative. Then it is followed by a prayer such as, "Here I am, send me."

Juanita wrote in *A Key Encounter* newsletter in March 2018 that she was working on the free mobile blood-pressure screening van (I remind you again she is in her 80s) when a well-dressed professional woman came onto the van with tears on her face telling everyone who would listen, "I am tired of depression...tired of the pills...my depression has gone on for years, I will never be free of this!" Juanita interrupted her and said, "Please don't say that! You can be free! I can understand what you're saying. My depression went on for several years when I was a young mother. But I learned that I can be free of depression and YOU can be free, too."

The two ladies spoke together for some time and prayed together. The lady left the van saying, "I reject thinking and saying I cannot get past this depression. I will give God permission to help me. I'm choosing to believe Him. Thank you, thank you, thank you. I will read this *Power to Cope* magazine you have given me. I do reject the thought that I will never be free. I am choosing to believe God has set me free. I can live without depression."

Another person, whose name escapes me now, shared with me a Bible text that helped her through a discouraging time: *"You will keep him in perfect peace, whose mind is stayed on you, because he trusts in You"* (Isaiah 26:3). This person read this verse over and over again, but each time personalized it, emphasizing a different word. The first time she read it as: "YOU, THE GOD OF THE UNIVERSE, will keep me in perfect peace as my mind is stayed on You, because I trust in You." Then: "You WILL MOST DEFINITELY keep me in perfect peace as my mind is stayed on You, because I trust in You." Followed by: "You will KEEP me CONTINUALLY AND FOREVER in perfect peace as my mind is stayed on You, because I trust in You." One more example: "You will keep ME, EVEN ME, Jeff Zaremsky, in perfect peace as my mind is stayed on You, because I trust in You." You get the idea.

If you really believe what you are reading when you are reading God's Word, it will be hard to remain discouraged.

If you are having trouble really believing, ask God to give you faith to believe, just as one person in the Bible prayed, *"Lord, I believe; help my unbelief!"* (Mark 9:24). God gives to everyone a measure of faith. If you need more, just ask Him for it.

It is very powerful to read God's Word, personalizing it, and giving it immediate application to what you are going through. If you are feeling low or going through a time when you are troubled, fearful, anxious, or worried, I encourage you to claim Bible verses right now and read them over and over again, personalizing them and emphasizing a different word each time you read them.

PAUSE, PONDER, AND PROCEED

1. Did you, like David, experience rejection as a child? If so, I am sorry to hear that. It is my prayer that you will be encouraged that just as David did not allow his rejection as a child to keep him from

being king of Israel, you also will not let the past wrongs of others stop you from being all that God has called you to be.

2. If you are currently in a "pit" or crying through the night or have external enemies or internal guilt, write your own psalm. It does not have to be poetic, it does not have to rhyme or be musical (although it can be if God has given you those talents); just make sure that in addition to writing the problems, surround them and overwhelm them with words of praise to God, words of faith, and words of hope.

3. If you are involved in a relationship where you are being abused physically or mentally, and you are excusing staying in the relationship because you have forgiven the person, I encourage you to ask God to give you the power to move (physically if necessarily) far enough away out of the relationship so that you are not being abused, while at the same time asking God to give you a heart of true forgiveness toward the abuser.

4. If the guilt of your sins are weighing you down, reread Psalm 51 out loud and personalize it with your name in it. And then claim His promise that you are now *a new creation; old things have passed away; behold, all things have become new.*

5. If you are prone to reject instruction or be insulted by correction, ask God to give you humility to learn

and hear from God and whomever He chooses to use to help you.

6. If you feel like you can't go on for another minute, get a watch and pray for God to sustain you for five more minutes and continue that every five minutes, with other prayers, until hope is revived.

7. If you are facing a problem that is way beyond your control (like being in an ambulance with pancreatitis, or whatever problem you are going through), ask God to make you His missionary through this experience. Ask Him to use you in witnessing for Him to everyone the problem brings you in contact with.

8. If you have been telling yourself and others that you will never be freed from depression, choose to reject those thoughts. Choose to believe God will set you free, that you can live, by His power, without depression. (If you are on doctor-prescribed medication for depression, do not take yourself off. As you bring down your hit levels you can ask your doctor about weaning you off the medications.)

9. Read or write out this verse several times, each time emphasize and personalize a different word in the verse: "You, Lord, will keep me in perfect peace, as my mind is stayed on You, because I trust in You."

Notes

1. Juanita Kretchmar's story was adapted with permission from the booklet, *Only by Love.*

2. Used with permission from the A Key Encounter newsletter, June 2016.

9

KING SAUL— KING OF FEAR

KING SAUL WAS THE FIRST KING OF ISRAEL, IMMEDIATELY preceding King David. His is a very sad story with an important lesson for us all, no matter what our position in life.

Israel was led by prophets and judges, but when the people wanted to be like the other nations, God granted their wish and had the prophet Samuel anoint Saul to be king.

At first Saul shied away from the position, even hiding from the prophet and the people when his name was called. This action portrays either a fear or insecurity. True humility would have accepted the call, all the while knowing it was God who called, God who gave the abilities, and God who gave the successes.

Saul was filled with God's Spirit after his anointing by Samuel. God gave Saul a new heart and God even caused Saul to prophesy. But when confronted with an attacking army, Saul allowed his fears to cause him to not wait upon the Lord. Instead of waiting for Samuel to come and intercede on behalf of the nation and offer the sacrifice, Saul offered the sacrifice himself. When Samuel arrived he sternly rebuked Saul.

Another time Samuel gave Saul strict instructions regarding what to do about a certain enemy nation. Instead of wiping them out as Samuel instructed, Saul let their king live and let the people keep the choicest animals for themselves. When Samuel met Saul, Saul gave excuses for his actions. Samuel, under the direction of God, told Saul that the kingdom would be taken from him and given to another. Yet God continued to allow Saul to remain king for many years after that.

After Saul's blatant and open disobedience and lack of true repentance, *"the Spirit of the Lord departed from Saul, and a distressing spirit from the Lord troubled him."* When the Bible says *"a distressing spirit of the Lord troubled him,"* it could be a reference to God convicting Saul and Saul being distressed by guilt for his actions or distressed by his anger at God because God promised to take the kingdom from him.

> *Saul's servants said to him, "...Let our master now command your servants, who are before you, to seek out a man who is a skillful player on the harp. And it shall be that he will play it with his hand when the distressing spirit from God is upon you, and you shall be well." So Saul said to his servants, "Provide me now a man who*

can play well, and bring him to me." Then one of the servants answered and said, "Look, I have seen a son of Jesse the Bethlehemite, who is skillful in playing, a mighty man of valor, a man of war, prudent in speech, and a handsome person; and the Lord is with him." Therefore Saul sent messengers to Jesse, and said, "Send me your son David, who is with the sheep." ...And so it was, whenever the spirit from God was upon Saul, that David would take a harp and play it with his hand. Then Saul would become refreshed and well, and the distressing spirit would depart from him (1 Samuel 16:14-19,23).

There is no doubt some types of music will make us more edgy and irritable. But music that has a soothing melody and rhythm, and godly words, can be very calming and helpful.

An article in *USA Today* titled, "20 Surprising, Science-Backed Health Benefits of Music" listed among the 20 health benefits that music reduces stress, eases pain, improves quality sleep, elevates mood, reduces anxiety, and relieves symptoms of depression.[1]

As we listen to godly music, the melody can soothe, motivate, or inspire us. The words can give us insight, hope, strength, courage, and encouragement. Words have a way of sticking in our minds better when connected with music.

One night I was driving home from a meeting where I was viciously and unjustly, verbally attacked by a group of "godly" people. It was horrible. I was totally taken off guard and felt like I had been ambushed. On the ride home I struggled with my thoughts as I allowed God to search my heart to see if any of their accusations were true, and also tried to cope with the manner in which their accusations were thrown at me. As my mind was thus stirred, I suddenly realized a song was running through my mind over and over again. It began to flow out of my mouth, "Draw me nearer, nearer blessed Lord to thy precious bleeding side." I started to sing it louder and louder.

At first I felt comfort in the thought of drawing nearer to the Lord, but then it hit me for the first time that the song does not say draw me nearer to Your strong arms or to Your comforting hug, but "to Your bleeding side"! It dawned on me that the only way to get to the Lord's comforting hug is by relating to His bleeding. He suffered much worse than I did and He was much more innocent than I am and He did it because of my sins. I found comfort in this experience, which helped me in a small way understand the unjust suffering He endured for me when He walked this earth.

If you are being attacked right now, or if you have been attacked in the past and you have not gotten over it yet, I pray this song and thought will help you appreciate that you have been found worthy to suffer as He suffered so you can understand His suffering for you a little better.

Like music, laughter can help us in our troubles. King Solomon wrote there is *"A time to weep, and a time to laugh; a time to mourn, and a time to dance"; "A merry heart makes a cheerful countenance, but by sorrow of the heart the spirit is broken"; "A merry heart does good, like medicine, but a broken spirit dries the bones"* (Ecclesiastes 3:4; Proverbs 15:13; Proverbs 17:22).

Some people believe maintaining a sense of humor helped some survivors through the Holocaust. Chaya Ostrower discovered while interviewing 84 Holocaust survivors for her doctoral thesis that "humor in the Holocaust fulfilled all the functions of humor, but especially that of Defense Mechanism, including its sub types—Self-humor and Gallows humor." One survivor interviewed for the study said, "the reason I survived...was laughter and humor...." Another survivor said, "Humor was one of the integral ingredients of mental perseverance. ...it was very important, very important. Humor and satire played a tremendous role, in my opinion."[2]

I like to laugh and joke around. One time I was telling a friend about a horrible experience I had been through and was still going through. She said, "Well I'm glad you are able to laugh about it." I had not even realized I was laughing. Even though the experience was causing me tremendous pain, I was telling it in a humorous way, plus the ridiculousness of it all struck me as, "This would be very funny if it wasn't real," and I was laughing as I told the story.

One time, among many, I showed up to a meeting late. I apologized for being late. Someone at the meeting said, "No need to apologize, this is the time you usually get here." I burst out laughing and said, "Then I guess I'm on time." I could have taken offense to the statement. I could have gotten angry. I could have attacked and pointed out their faults. I could have given all my excuses for my "tardiness." I could have gotten sullen that I was embarrassed in front of everyone. I could have said to myself, "I am a failure, no one likes me." I could have tried to invoke the sympathy of the others who heard the "attack" on poor me. I guess I could have also taken the statement to heart and tried to be on time next time. But the point is, I chose to laugh instead of resorting to any of the negative options (or the positive one) I had before me. And I chose to take the rebuke as a kindness to help me not be rude and insensitive to other people's time.

I was physically attacked, knocked to the ground, choked, and threatened with being killed by someone 20 years younger than me, literally twice my weight, and a good 13 inches (that is over a foot for those who are not good at math) taller than me. My wife even had a picture of him choking me out on a public street. Fortunately he let me go. I called the police, told my story, and showed them the picture. After the giant told the police that he was defending himself from me, they read me my Miranda Rights and threatened to arrest me. I started to unconsciously laugh spontaneously—not a good thing to do in front of a police officer. One of the officers said, "This is not funny." I sobered up quickly and replied, "No, it is not; it is ridiculous." True, but probably not the best thing to say at that moment. Laughing at that time might not have been a great idea, but it was my coping mechanism kicking in.

There are times when my lovely wife gets to scolding me about something and I start laughing. This, of course, makes her even more upset with me, which causes me to laugh even harder, sometimes even rib-hurting laughter. I believe this sense of humor that God has given me has helped me cope with some of the difficulties I have been through. I also believe it has been the cause of my sleeping on the couch a few times (which really isn't too bad; it's kind of like camping ☺).

But laughter alone is not enough to give us power to cope. There have been some very funny people who have committed suicide. We will see music is not always enough either.

Back to the life of Saul. Goliath, a nine-and-a-half-foot tall giant with six fingers on each hand, and the army of the Philistines threatened Israel. *"When Saul and all Israel heard these words of the Philistine, they were dismayed and greatly afraid"* (1 Samuel 17:11). As we read through the forty or so years of recorded history of Saul's life, we see fear popping up several times. He was fearful of being king, then he was fearful of Goliath, no doubt with good reason on both accounts. But life is full of fears, real and imaginary. We cannot let fear incapacitate us. Real fear is overcome with real faith, faith in God that He is more powerful than anything we are fearful of.

Long story short, young David came along and killed the giant that had Saul paralyzed with fear.

> *David went out wherever Saul sent him, and behaved wisely. Saul set him over the men of war, and he was accepted in the sight of all the people and also in the sight of Saul's servants. Now it had happened, when David was returning from the slaughter of the Philistine, that the women came out of all the cities of Israel, singing and dancing, to meet King Saul, with tambourines, with joy, and with musical instruments. So the women sang as they danced, and said, "Saul has slain his thousands, and David his ten thousands." Then Saul was very angry, and the saying displeased him; and he said, "They have ascribed to David ten thousands, and to me they have ascribed only thousands. Now what more can he have but the kingdom?" So Saul eyed David from that day forward* (1 Samuel 18:5-9).

Saul was fearful again, not of the giant Goliath taking his life, but of David taking his place. This fear led to jealousy, suspicion, and anger.

> *It happened on the next day that the distressing spirit from God came upon Saul.... So David played music with his hand, as at other times; but there was a spear in Saul's hand. And Saul cast the spear, for he said, "I will pin David to the wall!" But David escaped his presence twice. Now Saul was afraid of David, because the Lord was with him, but had departed from Saul* (1 Samuel 18:10-12).

The music did not work this time when Saul was filled with anger, jealousy, and fear. I doubt a joke by David would have worked at this point either. *"But all Israel and Judah loved David..."* (1 Samuel 18:16).

King Saul hoped that David would die at the hands of the Philistines. Saul offered David his daughter's hand in marriage for 100 foreskins of the Philistines (if you don't know what the foreskin is, I am not going to tell you). David took it upon himself to double the price and his men brought Saul 200 foreskins (pretty sick if you ask me, but I am just telling the story). *"Saul saw and knew the Lord was with David, and that Michal, Saul's daughter, loved him; and Saul was still more afraid of David. Saul became David's enemy continually"* (1 Samuel 18:28-29).

David did nothing wrong to Saul. David was not trying to take Saul's throne. Everything David did for Saul was good. David was fighting for Saul, not against him. Interestingly, fear of David's success (jealousy) led Saul to become the enemy of David.

Sometimes people who were our friends become jealous of us and then become our enemies even if we did not do anything wrong to them. Sometimes the reason we are angry at people is because we are jealous of them, not because they did anything intentional against us. Jealousy, anger, and fear lead us down dangerous paths. As we will see with Saul, it's sometimes a fateful path.

Saul tried to get his son Jonathan and his servants to kill David, but Jonathan talked him out of it. David again went to war and came back successful. David was back at the king's palace again:

> *Now the distressing spirit from the Lord came upon Saul as he sat in his house with his spear in his hand. And David was playing music with his hand. Then Saul sought to pin David to the wall with the spear, but he slipped away from Saul's presence; and he drove the spear into the wall. So David fled and escaped that night* (1 Samuel 19:9-10).

The next time Jonathan tried to defend David before his father:

> *Saul's anger was aroused against Jonathan, and he said to him, "You son of a perverse, rebellious woman! Do I not know that you have chosen the son of Jesse to your own shame and to the shame of your mother's nakedness? For as long as the son of Jesse lives on the earth, you shall not be established, nor your kingdom. Now therefore, send and bring him to me, for he shall surely die." And Jonathan answered Saul his father, and said to him, "Why should he be killed? What has he done?" Then Saul cast a spear at him to kill him, by which Jonathan*

knew that it was determined by his father to kill David
(1 Samuel 20:30-33).

I think I would have known that before I had a spear thrown at me. Or maybe not. We can so deceive ourselves regarding our own condition and that of our loved ones that we might not always readily see how low we have fallen. It is helpful to get an outside opinion once in a while.

Did you notice in the last paragraph that Saul did not refer to David by his name but rather as "the son of Jesse." Have you ever been so angry at someone that you can't even say the person's name, but rather refer to this person by some other, sometimes nasty, names? I know there have been times when I have been hurt by someone and if someone else mentioned this person's name the word "putz" automatically popped into my head. Sometimes the person was not even referring to "my" nemesis, but just someone else with the same name as the person I chose to be angry at, and yet it reminded me of the person who hurt me, sometimes months after the initial hurt, yet the anger still showed itself again.

Time alone will not remove anger or hurt. It needs to be confessed to God so the Messiah's death can remove it from us. This does not excuse their wrong, nor release the wrongdoers from being punished, but it releases us from choosing to hold on to anger or hurt, which will only destroy us.

In Saul and David's case, David did no wrong, yet Saul chose to be jealous and angry. David beautifully and successfully kept from retaliating and being angry by trusting in God and forgiving Saul.

I remember starting a new job and being introduced to some of the workers when one person said, "Oh no, not another Jeff." She didn't even know me, but apparently there had been another Jeff who worked there, and this person did not like him. Anger at one person can cause us to take it out on other people. By God's grace I successfully worked very hard to gain this person's friendship and hopefully saved the name for all the other Jeffs she might run into in the future.

Sometime after Saul threw a spear at his own son, he fell so low as to kill a group of Levites who gave David some bread. Have you ever been angry at someone just because that person was nice to someone with whom you were angry? Have you ever kicked the proverbial cat out of anger at someone else? Have you ever been short-tempered, mean, or discourteous toward your spouse or your children because you had a bad day at work or school? Thankfully there is forgiveness in the grace of Messiah and God can give us humility to confess those actions to the ones we hurt.

Anger and depression can be the opposite sides of the same coin. We get angry with those we feel we have power over; we get depressed when we feel we have no power over the situation.

That is why we keep our mouths shut in front of our bosses, bullies, or some authority figures who can cause us harm, but yell at our spouse, children, work subordinates, or other people we feel we have power over or think will not be able to retaliate against us.

When Saul felt he was in a position of power over David and over the Levites, he persecuted them. In a few more paragraphs we will see that when he came in contact with a power he felt was bigger than he was, Saul became depressed.

If we have a healthy fear of the Lord we will treat others as we want to be treated, we will not take out our anger on others for we know that God takes pity on the "little" ones, and we will realize that we are all under God's authority. Thus, no one is greater or lesser than we are—we are all equal under Him—so we don't have to fear the "big powers over us" nor do we have to take out our frustrations on others. Thankfully, we can surrender all our fears and aggravations to the Lord and not become angry or depressed.

After killing the Levites, Saul continued his anger toward David, even chasing him around the country. David showed time and time again that he had forgiven Saul and was not angry at him. Saul relented from time to time, but then picked up the anger and jealousy again.

Eventually Saul gave up on chasing David, possibly because a larger problem presented itself—the Philistines were attacking Israel again. And Saul made a huge mistake. Fear gripped Saul again. God had stopped speaking with him. As the psalm says, *"If I regard iniquity in my heart, the Lord will not hear"* (Psalm 66:18).

The prophet Samuel had died and God was not speaking to Saul through any other prophet or any other means. So feeling fearful and desperate, Saul went to a witch. Saul knew that going to a witch was wrong, yet he did it anyway. The witch did her thing and an apparition of what they believed to be the prophet Samuel came up from the earth.

Note that it is clear that it was not Samuel for many reasons. If God was not willing to speak to Saul at that point because of his refusal to give up his sinful attitudes, then God would not listen to a witch and allow a witch to have Samuel speak to Saul. Also Solomon told us that the dead have no more part in anything that takes place on the earth (Ecclesiastes 9:6). And Moses told us not to talk to the dead (Leviticus 19:31; 20:6). And the message that came from the apparition was nothing but doom, not a trace of hope for redemption—thus it was not a message from God. This apparition was no doubt a fallen evil angel (a demon) impersonating Samuel.

Saul was experiencing several depression hits, including a nutritional hit as he was not eating well, a circadian rhythm hit as he was not sleeping well, a frontal lobe hit as he was dealing with guilt brought on by wrong choices that he did not repent of, and a social hit as he felt isolated from God, and because of his behavior he was pushing others away from him.

Saul went into battle without any sleep and with thoughts of despair, believing that all his sons and he were going to die. This became a self-fulfilling prophecy. The Philistines routed Israel and killed Saul's sons and injured Saul. Saul, fearful of what was going to happen to him, fell on his sword and killed himself.

What a sad end to such a promising life.

It is sadly ironic how the people wanted a king to keep them from being afraid. They were pleased to have a strong man who was head and shoulders taller than everyone else. But height and human might are helpless in the face of fear. No matter what we have on this earth to give us a sense of security, only God gives us peace and courage in the face of danger. David, a small youth, feared the Lord, thus he did not fear Goliath. Saul, a big man, trusted in his own abilities, and he was filled with fears.

Fear led to anger and jealousy, and to despair and hopelessness. If you are experiencing any of those five destructive feelings, surrender them to God. Confess them as sin, as lacking faith in God and His Word. Accept His forgiveness and deliverance and His power to have hope, faith, courage, and strength.

The Bible calls us to fear the Lord. Solomon said, *"The fear of the Lord is the beginning of knowledge* [wisdom]" (Proverbs 1:7). But this is a different fear from the Goliaths in our lives. Fear of the Lord is a respect for His awesome power. But more than that, a fear of the Lord is a fear of hurting Him and letting Him down, a fear of *crucifying Him afresh* (see Hebrews 6:6 KJV).

A youth was always being nagged by his mother regarding his drug use. One day he came home stoned. He waited for his mother's tirade, but she looked at him and started to cry and ran into her room crying. That was the last time he did drugs, not because he feared hurting himself or being punished, but he feared breaking his mother's heart. When we fear the Lord, because of His great love for us, we will not want to sin and hurt Him.

When we fear the Lord because of His awesome power, we don't have to fear anything else because He is awesome in power and because He is on our side. He is more than a match for anything that attacks us.

Various fears will raise themselves up throughout our lives, but we can remember that, *"God has not given us a spirit of fear, but of power and of love and of a sound mind"* (2 Timothy 1:7). What a wonderful promise to claim over and over again.

Saul and David's lives have some similarities. Both were kings of Israel, both were anointed by God, both had very real issues facing them with very real fears and very real troubles. Both made some terribly bad mistakes. Saul chose to rely on his own strength and abilities, and on those of other people. David chose to rely on

God and use his God-given talents and abilities, and benefit from the strengths and abilities that God blessed other people with. Saul chose not to repent of his sin. David chose to accept rebuke and he repented. Saul chose to be angry and vengeful. David chose to forgive. Saul chose to be afraid. David chose to trust God.

While we have all made mistakes like Saul and David, and we all have very real fears to face, we can choose to follow Saul's example or David's. Whose example do you choose to follow?

Pause, Ponder, and Proceed

1. If you are mentally or emotionally under attack, or if the same worries or fears keep rehearsing in your mind, choose a godly song and sing it out loud (even if your voice is as bad as mine) until the negative thoughts that have been occupying your mind no longer have center stage.

2. If you are feeling down in the dumps, watch a good, clean humorous movie or show. It won't solve your problem, but it could cheer you up a little and clear your head of the stinking thinking long enough to help you think realistically about what is the root of your feelings.

3. Can you think of a time when you stuffed anger because you chose to get angry at someone who was in a position of strength, only to unstuff that anger and let it out on someone who you felt would not attack you back, such as your family, friend, or someone you considered in a weaker position than you?

If so, ask God to give you the gift of repentance, humility, and contrition, and go and apologize to that person—even if it was a long time ago. Doing so will be good for both you and them.

4. If you are feeling depressed because you feel powerless regarding the situation you are going through, claim these promises (or any of the hundreds in the Bible like them), *"Do not be afraid. Stand still, and see the salvation of the Lord. ...The Lord will fight for you, and you shall hold your peace"* (Exodus 14:13-14). *"Unto the upright there arises light in the darkness; he is gracious, and full of compassion, and righteous. A good man deals graciously and lends; he will guide his affairs with discretion. Surely he will never be shaken; the righteous will be in everlasting remembrance. He will not be afraid of evil tidings; his heart is steadfast, trusting in the Lord. His heart is established; he will not be afraid, until he sees his desire upon his enemies"* (Psalm 112:4-8). At the presence of the Lord *"the mountains shall be thrown down, the steep places shall fall, and every wall shall fall to the ground"* (Ezekiel 38:20).

5. If you are experiencing fear, anger, jealousy, despair, or hopelessness, surrender them to God. Confess them as sin, as lacking faith in God and His Word. Accept His forgiveness and deliverance and His power to have hope, faith, courage, and strength.

NOTES

1. Scott Christ, "20 surprising, science-backed health benefits of music," USAToday.com, December 17, 2013; https://www .usatoday.com/story/news/health/2013/12/17/health -benefits -music/4053401/; accessed October 21, 2020.

2. Chaya Ostrower, "Humor as a defense mechanism in the Holocaust," Thesis at Tel-Aviv University for Doctor of Philosophy degree; January 2000; https://remember.org/ humor; accessed October 21, 2020.

10

JEREMIAH—THE CRYING PROPHET

THE PROPHET JEREMIAH WROTE TWO BOOKS OF THE BIBLE. One of them is Lamentations, because he had much to lament and be sad about. As with many of the people listed in the Bible, his problems were not imaginary fears or worries about possible difficulties in the future. His problems were real and he was experiencing them daily. Jeremiah prophesied for a long time, about forty years, under some tremendous difficulties. Jeremiah was of Levitical descent and was called to serve in the Temple.

Throughout the very long book of the Bible titled under his name, which spans the time of at least five kings, Jeremiah wrote about the coming judgment of God that would allow Babylon to destroy Jerusalem and either kill or take captive almost everyone. This was definitely not a pleasant job.

Early on God told Jeremiah that he was not going to be allowed to have a wife or children. There are only a few names of people who stood with him or believed him. His parents and siblings are never mentioned. He must have been very lonely—a social hit.

Throughout this long period of time he was persecuted, harassed, beaten, threatened, misquoted, falsely accused, thrown in prison, thrown into a deep, dirty, wet pit and left to die (but was saved out of it), while his writings were ripped up and burned; and you thought you were having a bad day. He lived through a time when the city he was living in, Jerusalem, was under siege with no food coming in. Bare necessities, even daily bread, were scarce to non-existent. The prophet Ezekiel said cannibalism was taking place in the city during that time (Ezekiel 5:10). In other words, things were really, really bad in a way that you and I can't fathom, unless we have lived through it. You no doubt can recognize several depression hits that would come from living under those types of circumstances.

Very typical of how we feel when we are depressed, Jeremiah felt like his problem was worse than anyone else's in the world and no one else could relate to how bad his situation was. *"See if there is any sorrow like my sorrow"* (Lamentations 1:12). His situation was much worse than some people today experience, although sadly there are areas of the world that still suffer this badly even today. When he wrote the book of Lamentations, he had just gone through the third siege of his city, the last one of the three, which lasted one and a half years and ended with the entire city, including God's Temple, destroyed. All around Jeremiah young women had been raped, children were eaten, old men were beaten, young men were enslaved, and many were killed or were dying of disease. Most of us can't fathom living through such a time.

Maybe you can relate to some of these feelings Jeremiah expressed in the hauntingly sad book of Lamentations. The first word of the first, second, and fourth chapters is the word "How," as if Jeremiah is crying out in despair throughout the book, "How can this possibly be happening to us?" No doubt you, like I, have cried out that prayer many times in our lives. The Hebrew word for *how* is *ehkah*. That is the name of the book in Hebrew versions of the Bible.

Describing his city, Jerusalem, Jeremiah wrote:

She weeps bitterly in the night, her tears are on her cheeks; among all her lovers she has none to comfort her. All her friends have dealt treacherously with her; they have become her enemies. ...Her adversaries have become the master, her enemies prosper; for the Lord has afflicted her because of the multitude of her transgressions. Her children have gone into captivity before the enemy. ...In the days of her affliction and roaming, Jerusalem remembers all her pleasant things that she had in the days of old. When her people fell into the hand of the enemy, with no one to help her, the adversaries saw her and mocked her downfall. ...They have heard that I sigh, but no one comforts me. All my enemies have heard of my trouble; they are glad that You have done it. Bring on the day You have announced, that they may become like me (Lamentations 1:2,5,7,21).

Have you sometimes felt like all your friends have dealt treacherously with you, that there was no one to comfort you? Have you wept bitterly in the night? Have your "enemies" ruled over you? Has any of it been because of your own mistakes? Have your children been separated from you? Have you lost many of the pleasant things that you once owned? Have people mocked at your downfall? Have you ever desired that other people would suffer like you are so that you would not be suffering alone, or so that they would be punished for hurting you? If so, then you can relate to Jeremiah. But let's not stop there, because Jeremiah found a way out.

Through all his sorrows Jeremiah never forgot God. However, at times he blamed God for the calamities he knew were the result of his people's sins.

> *I am the man who has seen affliction by the rod of His wrath. He has led me and made me walk in darkness and not in light. Surely He has turned His hand against me time and time again throughout the day. He has aged my flesh and my skin, and broken my bones. He has besieged me and surrounded me with bitterness and woe. He has set me in dark places like the dead of long ago. He has hedged me in so that I cannot get out; He has made my chain heavy. Even when I cry and shout, He shuts out my prayer. He has blocked my ways with hewn stone; He has made my paths crooked. He has been to me a bear lying in wait, like a lion in ambush.*
>
> *He has turned aside my ways and torn me in pieces; He has made me desolate. He has bent His bow and set me up as a target for the arrow. He has caused the arrows*

of His quiver to pierce my loins. I have become the ridicule of all my people—their taunting song all the day. He has filled me with bitterness, He has made me drink wormwood. He has also broken my teeth with gravel, and covered me with ashes. You have moved my soul far from peace; I have forgotten prosperity. And I said, "My strength and my hope have perished from the Lord." Remember my affliction and roaming, the wormwood and the gall. My soul still remembers and sinks within me (Lamentations 3:1-20).

Pretty sad stuff, right? And this is coming from a prophet of the Lord who had been doing everything right and whom God liked. Fortunately Jeremiah did not let his thoughts stop there; he added:

This I recall to my mind, therefore I have hope. Through the Lord's mercies we are not consumed, because His compassions fail not. They are new every morning; great is Your faithfulness. "The Lord is my portion," says my soul, "Therefore I hope in Him!" The Lord is good to those who wait for Him, to the soul who seeks Him. It is good that one should hope and wait quietly for the salvation of the Lord. It is good for a man to bear the yoke in his youth. Let him sit alone and keep silent, because God has laid it on him; let him put his mouth in the dust— there may yet be hope. Let him give his cheek to the one who strikes him, and be full of reproach. For the Lord will not cast off forever. Though He causes grief, yet He will show compassion according to the multitude of His mercies. For He does not afflict willingly, nor grieve the children of men. ...Let us search out and examine our ways, and turn back to the Lord; let us lift our hearts and hands to God in heaven (Lamentations 3:21-33,40-41).

At least at one point Jeremiah wished he had never been born. His wishing he was dead is recorded prior to both the destruction of the city and the particular episode of depression we just read about in Lamentations. The wild ride that led up to his suicidal desire is very revealing. This account is found in Jeremiah chapter 20.

Pashhur the son of Immer, the priest who was also chief governor in the house of the Lord, heard that Jeremiah prophesied these things [the coming destruction of Jerusalem]. Then Pashhur struck Jeremiah the prophet, and put him in the stocks that were in the high gate of Benjamin, which was by the house of the Lord (Jeremiah 20:1-2).

What a way to start your day, by being beaten and locked up, possibly in a public square where others could mock you or hit you. Then, *"the next day Pashhur brought Jeremiah out of the stocks."* Wasn't that nice of him. What would you do at this point? Beg for mercy and apologize for not being politically correct? Keep quiet and slink home? Let's look at what Jeremiah did:

Jeremiah said to him, "The Lord has not called your name Pashhur, but Magor-Missabib [fear on every side]. For thus says the Lord: 'Behold, I will make you a terror to yourself and to all your friends; and they shall fall by the sword of their enemies, and your eyes shall see it. I will give all Judah into the hand of the king of Babylon, and he shall carry them captive to Babylon and slay them with the sword. Moreover I will deliver all the wealth of this city, all its produce, and all its precious things; all the treasures of the kings of Judah I will give into the hand of their enemies, who will plunder them, seize them, and carry them to Babylon. And you, Pashhur, and all who dwell in your house, shall go into captivity. You shall go to Babylon, and there you shall die, and be buried there, you and all your friends, to whom you have prophesied lies'" (Jeremiah 20:3-6).

That is certainly not the most tactful way to win people over to his side. Maybe there have been times you wish you had the backing of "thus saith the Lord" to speak that way to some people, but then again it came with a price. What Jeremiah said is not the way to win friends, so why did Jeremiah say it?

Jeremiah felt compelled by God to tell the truth as a warning and to lead them away from the path of destruction they were on.

O Lord, You induced me, and I was persuaded; You are stronger than I, and have prevailed. I am in derision daily; everyone mocks me. For when I spoke, I cried out; I shouted, "Violence and plunder!" Because the word of the Lord was made to me a reproach and a derision daily. Then I said, "I will not make mention of Him, nor speak anymore in His name..." (Jeremiah 20:7-9).

Now we are starting to see the roller-coaster ride Jeremiah was riding at this point. His day started with being beaten and locked up to being mocked and taunted. The next day he was released, which was no doubt a welcomed relief. He stood boldly for God, secure in who he was, and sure of God's calling upon him. He told it like it was, regardless of the outcome, but then derided daily and mocked by everyone, Jeremiah decided not to speak for God anymore and started to isolate himself. This is only the beginning of the ride—down, down, up, up, down, down. This ride is revealed clearly in Jeremiah 20:9-13:

"But His word was in my heart like a burning fire shut up in my bones; I was weary of holding it back, and I could not." Up again. He had God's conviction and Spirit burning within him and he could not hold it in, he had to fulfill God's call upon his life and warn these people for their own good.

"I heard many mocking: "Fear on every side!"" That is exactly what he said Pashhur would be called. *"Report," they say, "and we will report it!" All my acquaintances watched for my stumbling, saying, "Perhaps he can be induced; then we will prevail against him, and we will take our revenge on him."* Down again as he heard the mocking and threats.

"But the Lord is with me as a mighty, awesome One. Therefore my persecutors will stumble, and will not prevail. They will be greatly ashamed, for they will not prosper. Their everlasting confusion will never be forgotten." Up again as he remembered God's power and omnipotence. His trust in God overrode the fears.

"O Lord of hosts, You who test the righteous, and see the mind and heart, let me see Your vengeance on them; for I have pleaded my cause before You." At this down point, Jeremiah wanted to see their destruction as Jonah did regarding Nineveh.

"*Sing to the Lord! Praise the Lord! For He has delivered the life of the poor from the hand of evildoers.*" Up again as He put his trust in God.

Then boom, seemingly out of nowhere Jeremiah said:

> *Cursed be the day in which I was born! Let the day not be blessed in which my mother bore me! Let the man be cursed who brought news to my father, saying, "A male child has been born to you!" Making him very glad. Let that man be like the cities which the Lord overthrew, and did not relent; let him hear the cry in the morning and the shouting at noon, because he did not kill me from the womb, that my mother might have been my grave, and her womb always enlarged with me. Why did I come forth from the womb to see labor and sorrow, that my days should be consumed with shame?* (Jeremiah 20:14-18).

The chapter ends on that sad, low note—but not the book.

In the next chapter, chapter 21 of the book of Jeremiah, the king sends Pashhur to Jeremiah to ask the Lord if He will have mercy on them. How interesting that the king and Pashhur ask that of Jeremiah. Since they had not repented of their sins against God, Jeremiah gave them the same answer he had been giving all along—Jerusalem will be destroyed and you will be killed.

Jeremiah bounced back after wishing he was never born. Jeremiah sucked it up, accepted his calling and lot in life, and continued doing what he was called to do.

One lesson I think we can learn from Jeremiah's life (and other people in this book), is that it is not unusual at times to think death would be preferable to life. I called a friend recently to offer my condolences and support after her brother died. She was at peace with his death while coping with the loss. Then she said something surprising, "He is the fortunate one, he gets to rest until the Lord returns, the rest of us still have work to do. People think I'm nuts when I say things like that. I am not depressed or suicidal, that is just reality. I do miss him like my siblings do, I am just saying his work is done, ours continues on. It is not easy here on earth; while there are many blessings here, there is also plenty of sickness, troubles, pain, trials, and heartache. My brother at least does not have to experience any more of that." Paul put grieving the loss of a loved one this way, we *"sorrow not"* regarding those who are asleep, *"as others which have no hope"* (1 Thessalonians 4:13 KJV).

Many times I have likewise thought it would be easier to just take a short nap until the Lord returns rather than fight the good fight of faith here. Similarly, Paul wrote in another place:

> *It all accords with my earnest expectation and hope... as always, the Messiah will be honored by my body, whether it is alive or dead. For to me, life is the Messiah, and death is gain. But if by living on in the body I can do fruitful work, then I don't know which to choose. I am caught in a dilemma: my desire is to go off and be with the Messiah—that is better by far—but because of you, the greater need is to stay on in the body. Yes, I am convinced of this; so I know I will stay on with you in order to help you progress in the faith and have joy in it* (Philippians 1:20-25 CJB).

This does not mean that Paul, my friend, or I planned on committing suicide. It is just acknowledging that life on this earth can be horrible at times, and that God has a better place planned for those who love and follow Him. In the meantime, it is vitally important for us to make this horrible world a little bit more bearable for others, giving them hope and pointing them to the better place—heaven with God.

Sadness is normal under such circumstances. Depression is part of life sometimes and it needs to be worked through. But to try to numb sadness with alcohol, drugs, workaholism, busyness, rebound relationships, or other dysfunctional pseudo-coping mechanisms, only mask the symptoms and do not resolve the real issue. (I am not saying that there is no place at times for prescribed medications.) We deal with real sadness by facing it, accepting it, going through the stages of grief—denial, anger, blame, bargaining, and acceptance—and eventually moving on, trusting in the Lord in every stage.

While Jeremiah is referred to as the crying prophet (and he did cry a lot), most of his crying was not for himself, but for others. This is the key. After the destruction of Jerusalem, Jeremiah wrote, *"My eyes overflow with rivers of water for the destruction of the daughter of my people"* (Lamentations 3:48).

Pity parties don't get us anywhere other than making us lonelier because few people will want to be around us, and those who do stay with us are people who enjoy depressing pity parties because they feel the same way. That is no way to get out of a sad, depressed state. As motivational speaker Zig Ziglar said, "The problem with pity parties is that very few people come, and those who do come don't bring gifts." This is not to say that when we are going through a problem we should not find a confidant to counsel and feel free to unload on. But if that is all we can talk about, or if we talk about the problem freely with everyone, we will not be able to get the help we need.

One way to get out of a sad, depressed state is to stop looking at our own problems and start helping others get out of their problems, by caring for others instead of ourselves. That, of course, does not mean we ignore any real problems that need fixing in our lives, it just means we don't spend 24/7 focusing and worrying about our problems.

Jeremiah was facing and experiencing real problems. He went through his up and down roller coaster many times, yet he accepted his lot and focused on helping other people to receive the hope that is in the Lord.

In our natural, carnal state that we are born with, it is not possible to just stop thinking about ourselves and to start thinking about others. We are wired to be selfish. A baby does not say, "Mommy must be tired, I will wait until morning to cry for some milk." No, a baby says, "I want milk, I don't care about you, I only care about me, and I am going to cry until you give it to me." We have to teach our children to say please and thank you. Gratitude and unselfishness are not natural to us.

So how do we go from being self-absorbed to unselfish, from thinking only about ourselves and our needs and our problems, to caring about others? We confess our sins of selfishness and self-centeredness, and we accept the Messiah's sacrifice on our behalf for the death to that carnal nature, and we ask God to give us His mind, His thoughts, and His concern for others. Finally, we believe by faith that He has done that because He promised to do so. Since our carnal nature always tries to rise up again, and since satan taunts us to whine about ourselves, and because we will always have problems in this life, this type of prayer becomes a constant state of mind.

There is a difference between sympathy and empathy. And there is a time for both. Sympathy enters into the other person's suffering, feeling their pain, and crying with them. Empathy sees the other person's pain but does not enter into it with them, but rather stays outside so that they can help. If you have sympathy for people who are drowning, you will jump in the water with them, hug them, and drown with them. If you have empathy for people who are drowning, you stand on solid ground, throw them a rope, and pull them out of the water. Again, there are times for both. There are times to be sympathetic and just sit and cry with someone, even if the problem does not directly affect you. But other times it is better to be empathic.

Many times we borrow other people's problems and that makes us depressed. If our adult children are making wrong choices, messing up their lives, we don't have to drown with them. There is a time to stand on solid ground and throw them a rope, and there are times when they need to learn to swim. We need the Holy Spirit's guidance to know how to respond to their problems, but drowning with them is not one of them. If we drown with them, we will not be able to help them or anyone else.

My mother, Linda Brother, was depressed and attempted to commit suicide by ramming her car into a bridge. This was before airbags. The car was totaled. The tow truck driver could not believe anyone survived. Miraculously she walked away unhurt.

(That means I have a genetic hit). The book of Lamentations later became her favorite book in the Bible. Can you imagine a book with a title that basically says "crying" being someone's favorite book? Maybe you can. We will come back to that in a minute.

Linda was homeless, living in her car in New York City while in the midst of a court case she was losing. It was December and getting cold; she was driving down the Long Island expressway when she saw a large recreational vehicle painted white and blue with the letters, "Seventh-day Adventist Community Services." Being Jewish, she was not familiar with the religious organization, but she followed the van thinking that a community service organization could be of help to her. When the van pulled into a parking lot, several homeless people exited the van and walked toward the building. When Linda asked the driver if there was some way this organization could help her, she was invited inside for the party that was being held for the homeless people. Once inside, one of the staff prayed for her and invited her to stay for the party.

Linda could relate to the homeless people. Even though she was not sleeping on the streets, she was sleeping in her car and was homeless. She was amazed as she saw the food being served to the homeless people, the gifts that were given out, the hats and clothing that were shared. She heard the songs being sung and the testimonies of the staff that were told. Linda's heart was touched.

After the party, the homeless people went back on the vans, with all their gifts, to be taken back to the streets where they were picked up. Since Linda drove herself, she did not leave with the other homeless people. Instead, she stayed to help clean up as the staff began to minister personally to her. The community service center had some staff housing. They let Linda stay in one of the spare apartments. Linda was given a Bible and after a time of studying it, she committed her life to the Lord. God began His healing in her life, but she still had her struggles.

It was during this time of reading the Bible that the very sad book of Lamentations became her favorite book. She had it underlined everywhere and marked the margins with the dates she had cried through the night or when an injustice was done to her. When a friend of hers saw her markings in the book of Lamentations, he gave her a new Bible. He suggested that she put the past behind her, forgive those who had hurt her, accept God's new life for her, and move forward with God. Linda accepted his suggestion, and by God's grace she did so.

Linda had been on disability for depression, but God was healing her mind. She was able to get her own apartment and started working. Linda called social security and told them she no longer needed her disability payments for mental illness. The person on the phone said, "What are you crazy?" No, she was not crazy, she was being healed. It has been about thirty years since that time and Linda is still doing great and remains free of depression.

You too can be healed permanently. Commit your life to the Lord. Trust in Him. Accept His power to forgive those who have hurt you. Accept His sacrifice for the forgiveness of the mistakes you have made. Read His Word prayerfully each day. Let the Holy Spirit give you the power to obey God's Word. Let Him use you in serving and ministering to others. Get together regularly with others who are also committed to following and obeying the Lord. Let His Spirit empower you to move forward with the daily new life He has for you.

Behold what manner of love the Father has bestowed on us, that we should be called children of God! ...I know the thoughts that I think toward you, says the Lord, thoughts of peace and not of evil, to give you a future and a hope (1 John 3:1; Jeremiah 29:11).

Oh, and regarding the extremely sad Bible book that is so sad that translators titled it Lamentations, that was Linda's most marked-up book. It has become one of my favorite books of the Bible too, not because it is so sad, but because it is so amazing. It turns out that the book of Lamentations is much more than Jeremiah crying chapter after chapter as he gives horrid details of the destruction of Jerusalem. It is actually a divinely created poetic masterpiece with deep prophetic meaning. I have written a book entitled, *Lamentations, The Cry of Hope,* as a companion book to this book, *Depressed People of the Bible, How to Come Out of the Cave and into the Light. (Lamentations, The Cry of Hope* can be purchased at the same location where you bought *Depressed People of the Bible.)*

PAUSE, PONDER, AND PROCEED

1. If your life has been, or is currently, a roller-coaster ride of ups and downs, choose to accept God's current calling and purpose in your life.

2. If you are currently in one of the low parts of the roller-coaster track, choose to stand for God and represent Him properly in spite of the trials.

3. If you have been regularly holding pity parties, telling everyone within hearing range your problems,

choose not to bring up your problems except to one or two carefully picked people who have strong faith, are prayer warriors, are good listeners, who will not judge you or others, who are not gossips, and who will give you good advice—even if it is advice you might rather not hear. If you don't know someone who fits that description, ask your minister to recommend someone. If you don't regularly attend services and thus don't have a minister, I recommend you begin praying and working on finding a congregation you are happy with.

4. If you are in a situation, like Jeremiah in Jerusalem, where you are not the only one suffering, but you have only been thinking about how you are being effected, then confess to God your self-centeredness and ask God to give you a loving concern for the others who are in the same boat as you.

5. If you are now seeing—with Moses, Elijah, Jeremiah, Paul, my friend, me, etc.—that it is not abnormal to at times think it would have been better if you were never born or if the Lord took your life, then accept those thoughts for what they are, temptations from the devil, and move on with life. Make the best of it while you are in this world by serving God and directing more people to the Better Land.

6. When you are called to entrust someone else into God's hands, do you have the spiritual discernment to know when to be sympathetic, when to be empathic, when to let the other person grow and learn

on their own, and when to let someone else help them?

7. If you are receiving disability payments for mental illness, like Linda was, wouldn't you like to be able to call, like she did, and tell them that your doctor says you no longer need the money? If so, keep working on lowering the depression hits and keep your eye on that goal.

Martha and Mary— Stages of Grief

Martha and Mary experienced a type of sadness that almost all of us at one time or another experience—the loss of a loved one.

This account is recorded in the Gospels and concerns three Jewish people who became followers of Yeshua as the Messiah— His birth name is Yeshua. The angel of the Lord came to Joseph in a dream and told him that Mary *"will give birth to a son, and you are to name him Yeshua, [which means 'Adonai saves,'] because he will save his people from their sins"* (Matthew 1:21 CJB).

Solomon wrote, *"Better to go to the house of mourning than to go to the house of feasting, for that is the end of all men; and the living*

*will take it to heart. Sorrow is better than laughter, for by a sad coun-
tenance the heart is made better"* (Ecclesiastes 7:2-3).

Lazarus, Martha and Mary's brother, became sick. This account
is recorded in the Bible book of John chapter 11. The sisters sent a
message to Yeshua to come to them saying, *"Lord, behold, he whom
You love is sick"* (John 11:3). Even though Yeshua loved Lazarus,
He purposefully delayed a few days before going to Bethany where
this family lived.

Just before Yeshua came to Martha and Mary, He told His
disciples that Lazarus was sleeping. They thought He meant that
Lazarus was feeling better and was able to rest, but Yeshua was
referring to Lazarus' death, that he was sleeping in the grave, as in
dead, as in RIP—resting in peace.

When Yeshua arrived in Bethany, Lazarus had already been
dead four days. Martha and Mary were sitting shiva in the house
(more on that in the next chapter). When Martha heard Yeshua
was in Bethany, she came out and said to Him, *"Lord if you had
been here, my brother would not have died. But even now I know that
whatever You ask of God, God will give You."* Yeshua responded,
*"'Your brother will rise again.' Martha said to Him, 'I know that he
will rise again in the resurrection at the last day'"* (John 11:21-24).

When Mary came out to see Yeshua, she said, *"Lord, if You had
been here, my brother would not have died."* The exact same words
that Martha said. The two of them must have been saying it repeatedly to each other during those four days.

In a sense, Mary and Martha both blamed Yeshua and told
Him that He let them down, that He was not there for them when
they needed Him. When their brother was sick, He did not come,

and now their brother was dead. They had even sent a message for Him to come. He had no excuse. He blew it. Little did they know He had a reason for not being there and that it was going to work out for the greater good.

There are five distinct stages of grief. We can clearly see some of them in Martha and Mary from the account we have read so far. The five stages are denial, anger, blame, bargaining, and acceptance. The five stages are not in any particular order. None of us go through them in the same order, and even as we go through the stages we may go back and forth, leaving one stage only to come back to it again at a later time. There is no set duration for being in each stage, or set time we will emerge from the stages of grief. We can even be in more than one stage at once, or within minutes jump from one to another. It is different for everyone and for each type of grief. But we all experience these five at some point. The five stages of grief do not only apply to loss through death of a loved one, but any loss. It can be the loss of a limb, the ability to do something we used to do, the loss of a job, or the loss of a friend. It can even be as simple as when we can't find our keys.

Which ones do you see Martha and Mary experiencing in their story? Denial? "I can't believe he is dead, if only Yeshua had been here." Blame? "If You had been here my brother would not have died." Acceptance? "I know that he will rise again in the resurrection at the last day." Bargaining? "Yeshua, can You pray to the Father, I know He will give You whatever You ask."

In situational grieving sometimes we blame ourselves, sometimes we blame others, sometimes we blame the person or thing that we lost—sometimes we might even blame God. For example, "If I would have just done more, been there more often, said such and such," etc. Or we may blame other people; for example, "If it wasn't for that boss, if that doctor did..., etc." Or we might blame the person or thing; for example, "If they had only taken better care of themselves," or "If that car wasn't so rusted it would still be running now." Or "God could have prevented this."

Similarly, we can be angry with ourselves, someone else, or the person or thing we lost. Just as we can bounce around through the stages we can bounce around in who we are angry with or who we blame. We can be in several stages at the same time as we see in the statements that Martha made.

Denial can manifest in a simple statement like: "I can't believe he is gone." Or it can be coming home from work and expecting to see the person, only to remember a moment later that this person will not be there.

Acceptance doesn't only come at the end. We can start with acceptance only to go through the other stages afterward. We can move in and out of acceptance. Even when the other four stages aren't as strong any more, acceptance is not an absence of grief. We never really stop grieving large losses; the hole will always be there. Nothing can fill it, but we can come to a point of accepting the fact that he/she/they/it is not coming back. We start the next chapter of our lives. Even long after we have been living in acceptance, something can happen to reawaken the other stages, such as a birthday, anniversary, or some other reminder of the loss.

The reason to know all this is because it is helpful to know these feelings are normal and natural. We are not going *mashugana* (crazy), nor are we the only ones who feel and think this way. It is not wrong to ponder these thoughts and go through these stages.

Everyone experiences these stages of grief. It is not a lack of faith to experience the stages of grief. In actuality, the Lord gave us these processes to help our minds acclimate to loss. This is His design.

Going through the stages is very helpful. When we suppress the feelings of grief, we prolong the grief. When my grandfather on my mother's side died, my grandmother was understandably depressed after more than fifty years of marriage together. When she went to her doctor for her regular checkup, he asked how she was doing, and she told him she was depressed. He wanted to prescribe antidepressants for her. She declined. In this book I am not going to get into the pros and cons of medication, but I do want to point out here there is a difference between situational depression and clinical depression. It is normal to be depressed when we lose a loved one. Suppressing those feelings is a form of denial. The alcoholic might forget his/her problems during a night of drinking, but the problems are still there, and often worse in the morning. Trying to cover up our feelings of loss is not a good idea. It is best to acknowledge the stages, accept them for what they are—a stage in the grief process. Then trust that God still has a purpose and a plan for our lives.

The story about Martha and Mary continued, *"When Yeshua saw her [Mary] crying, and also the Judeans who came with her crying, he was deeply moved and also troubled"* (John 11:33 CJB). Then comes the shortest verse in the Bible, *"Yeshua cried"* (John 11:35 CJB). Yeshua was not weeping in grief for the loss of Lazarus, because He knew what He was about to do; rather, He was weeping for and with Mary, Martha, and the others who were grieving. How beautiful to know we are not alone when we are grieving, Yeshua is grieving with us. He is touched with the feelings of our infirmities. In all our *tzures* (troubles), He is troubled. Yeshua feels our pain and He cries our tears with us. He truly is Immanuel, God with us. It is okay and even good to cry. Even Yeshua cried, and He will hold us and cry with us in our grief.

After speaking with Martha and Mary, Yeshua asked that the stone be rolled away from the tomb/cave where Lazarus had been buried. Martha protested, saying Lazarus had been in the tomb four days and his body must already be decaying and must stink. Yeshua insisted, and they rolled away the stone. Yeshua prayed to the heavenly Father and then He cried out, *"Lazarus, come forth!"* (not come down, or come up, but come forth), and Lazarus came out of the grave still wrapped in burial clothes (John 11:43-44). It must have been amazing to see. Yeshua has power over the grave! Yeshua has power over physical death as well as emotional death. He can raise us out of our caves to new lives in Him.

It is worth noting that even though Lazarus was dead in the grave for four days, he did not write a book, or a chapter, or even a verse about his experience in death. No doubt he truly was resting in peace. As Solomon wrote, *"the dead know nothing"* (Ecclesiastes 9:5).

When we have faith in God we don't have to fear the grave. We can still miss our loved ones, we can still grieve, but if our loved ones had surrendered their lives to the Lord and accepted the Messiah's death on their behalf, and accepted God's Spirit into their lives to give them victory, power over sin, and new lives, then we have the assurance that we will see them again, as Martha said to Yeshua, on the last day at the resurrection. And even if they did not surrender their lives to God, we can still be at peace knowing a loving God has given them every opportunity necessary for them to be with Him for eternity and that the final choice was theirs.

Rabbi Paul gave us some thoughts to comfort us in our grief when he wrote:

> *Now we do not want you to be uninformed, brothers and sisters, about those who are asleep, so that you may not grieve like the rest who have no hope. For if we believe that Yeshua died and rose again, so with Him God will also bring those who have fallen asleep in Yeshua. For this we tell you, by the word of the Lord, that we who are alive and remain until the coming of the Lord shall in no way precede those who are asleep. For the Lord Himself shall come down from heaven with a commanding shout, with the voice of the archangel and with the blast of God's shofar, and the dead in Messiah shall rise first. Then we who are alive, who are left behind, will be caught up together with them in the clouds, to meet the Lord in the air—and so we shall always be with the Lord. Therefore encourage one another with these words* (1 Thessalonians 4:13-18 TLV).

> *Behold, I tell you a mystery: We shall not all sleep, but we shall all be changed—in a moment, in the twinkling of an eye, at the last shofar. For the shofar will sound, and the dead will be raised incorruptible, and we will be changed. For this corruptible must put on incorruptibility, and this mortal must put on immortality. But when this corruptible will have put on incorruptibility and this mortal will have put on immortality, then shall come to pass the saying that is written: "Death is swallowed up in victory. Where, O Death, is your victory? Where, O Death, is your sting?"* (1 Corinthians 15:51-55 TLV)

Pause, Ponder, and Proceed

1. Have you experienced the death of a loved one or some other significant loss in the last 12 months? Can you identify which stage of grief—denial, anger, blame, bargaining, acceptance—you are in right now? Can you remember being in the other stages? Have you suppressed and stuffed down any stages of grief?

2. If you are grieving any loss, take comfort in that Yeshua is grieving with you, He cares for you; He is touched with your very feelings. There is no joy that He does not enjoy with us, nor any tear that He does not shed with us.

3. If you have lost a loved one, take comfort in that Yeshua loves that person even more than you ever could. Have hope in the resurrection and in a fair, just, merciful judgment. God is on their side. They would have had to consciously, consistently, rebelliously, purposefully chosen to reject His free love and grace in order to miss out on heaven.

4. Are you looking forward to resurrection morning? I am. Let us be faithful and true until then.

A Surprising Example of Depression

Yeshua was depressed. That might surprise some people because Yeshua did not sin, but it is not so surprising when we remember depression in and of itself is not sin. He *"was in all points tempted as we are, yet without sin"* (Hebrews 4:15). Yeshua took on our flesh, from the seed of Abraham, from the seed of David, with all its frailties and inherited weaknesses. He felt our feelings and our troubles and our struggles, yet He did not allow Himself to yield to temptations or sin. Yeshua's depression, if we can call it that, was a situational depression. He was grieving the loss of a loved one. In some ways this chapter is a complement to the chapter about Martha and Mary.

Depression is not sin. Depression can be a result of several things, such as experiencing a loss. At times it is sinful attitudes that can lead to depression. But even in those cases, it is the sinful attitudes that are sin, not the depression. In those cases depression is only a symptom of the sin, not the sin itself. Holding on to bitterness or self-pity are sinful attitudes that can lead to depression, but it is the attitudes, not the depression, that is sinful.

Yeshua went off to a solitary place to mourn when He learned that His cousin, John (known as the immerser) was beheaded by King Herod. In Judaism, after the death of a loved one we traditionally "sit *shiva*," which literally means "sit for seven." During those seven days we take a break from our regular work and daily activities so that we have time to remember our loved one.

We begin the process of going through the five stages of grief mentioned in the previous chapter, and give other people a chance to visit us to show their love and to grieve with us. It is a good time to get out the pictures and to reminisce by ourselves and with our friends. Sitting *shiva* is a time to memorialize our loved one. It helps keep us from falling into the busy routine of life as if the loved one did not die. It keeps us from ignoring our pain, deferring or suppressing the grieving process. Sitting *shiva* helps cement the memory of our loved one in our minds. It gives honor to the deceased and healing to us.

Sitting *shiva* is not a time for us to serve our guests. We don't need to be entertaining at such a time. Ideally, they will bring food so that we don't have to worry about such things. They can even help with some of the cleaning and other daily tasks to make our lives a little easier.

While Yeshua was off in a solidary place sitting *shiva* with His disciples, a multitude came out to Him, not to grieve with Him, but to have their needs met. When Yeshua saw the great multitude He was *"moved with compassion for them, because they were like sheep not having a shepherd"* (Mark 6:34). We too can look for ways to help others as a means of moving on after the loss of a loved one, ideally after we are done sitting *shiva*. This lifts us out of our self-focus and gives purpose to our lives.

Jennifer Jill Schwirzer, LPC, shared the following story with me:

Early in my counseling practice, a friend asked me to train his fellow members how to do what I do. The event blessed so many people I began to conduct the training regularly. When some of my counseling clients signed up, I began to ask myself if that was okay. If they themselves were struggling, should they be helping other people? I wondered. Then I saw a miracle.

I'll call her Evie. She originally came as a client, and I treated her for depression. Or I should say I tried to treat her, because she really didn't improve. But she came to the Abide Helper Training in which I train people how to be helpers (as opposed to helpees). And then she dramatically improved.

I think her depression had gouged her self-respect. When she saw that she could still help other people, even though not fully recovered herself, her sense of value returned to her. And in the process of helping other people she saw ways out of her own depression.

We comfort others with the comfort we receive from God. But it doesn't always happen sequentially, as in, "God helped me, now I'll help you." In fact, because it distracts me from what may have become an unhealthy self-focus, me helping you can actually clear out the channel for God helping me.

Praised be God, Father of our Lord Yeshua the Messiah, compassionate Father, God of all encouragement and comfort; who encourages us in all our trials, so that we can encourage others in whatever trials they may be undergoing with the encouragement we ourselves have received from God (2 Corinthians 1:3-4 CJB).

If you'd like to seek counseling, coaching, or other help from Jennifer's qualified staff, contact abide.network.

Some other traditions in Judaism that help us in our grief include saying the mourner's *kaddish.* It is neither a mournful dirge, nor a prayer for the dead, but rather a praise to the Giver of Life. Giving praise to God, even in the face of death, is a healthy thing to do. We have already seen how God gave Job the ability to praise God even after learning all his sons and daughters had died.

Also at the funeral, mourners tear a cloth pinned to their garments, expressing how their hearts are torn. After the casket is lowered into the ground, the mourners place soil on the casket, putting a sense of closure on the reality before them. This helps them in saying goodbye to their loved one. The physical action of participating in the burial brings our minds into harmony with the reality before us. In a sense we are burying our loved one, not merely leaving it for someone else to do. We are participating. And as the dirt goes into the grave, a part of our heart goes with it. This helps begin the process of closure.

Another helpful tradition is putting up the memorial stone on or about the one-year anniversary of the person's death. A year later life has changed but our love has not. We have not forgotten our loved one, and are reminded of that clearly as we return to the burial site. This again helps to bring closure to our loss.

Every year on the anniversary of the death of our loved one we light the *yahrzeit* (year time) candle to remember the person who died, demonstrating that he/she is still alive in our hearts and minds.

None of these traditions are mentioned in the Bible. None are mandatory. But all of them are helpful as we go through the grieving process. They can give us the ability to physically, visually, and audibly walk through our loss. These traditions are intended to give us time to mourn our loss before returning to the necessary routine of life, and they help us to remember our loved one.

I was visiting a woman whose husband had just passed away from a massive heart attack. Her mother was there also, and she said some words that stuck with me. She told her daughter that life is like a book and she was now entering the next chapter in that book. It is not to be compared with the previous chapters, better or worse, just different. Life now would be different from before she got married, and different from while she was married. It would be a new chapter filled with God's plans for her life. Each stage of life is unique and has pros and cons. We can remember the past with its joys and sorrows. At the same time, we should not miss out on the joys and sorrows, the memories and the impact, that our lives can be making now.

Helping people through the grieving process can be difficult as it is hard to know the right thing to say. Words one person may find encouraging might be hurtful to someone else. Even a simple line such as, "At least they are no longer suffering" might be offensive to one person and comforting to another. Sometimes it is best just to be a good listener. Or if they don't want to talk, just to be there with them. Sometimes people will want to be alone, at other times they will want someone with them. Other times it is best just to go with their emotions and desires. If they want to talk, listen and affirm. If they want to be quiet, be quiet with them. If they want time alone, give them space, but occasionally let them know you are there for them when they are ready. In other words, mourn with those who mourn.

It seems that when we are grieving we become extra sensitive. Our emotions are all over the place and we are stressed and concerned about many things regarding our loss. If you have been hurt by someone's words or actions while you were mourning the loss of a loved one (or any type of loss), I encourage you to forgive them. Most of such efforts are well intentioned. Often the motive is more important than the message. If they were with you during your time of mourning, chances are their motive was to support you. Yes, they might have said or done something without thinking, but nonetheless, forgiving them will benefit you.

There are two instances in the Bible where God commanded a person not to show grief. It must have been a very hard experience for each of them. One was Moses' brother Aaron after both his sons died at the same time as a result of their sins. The other was Ezekiel when his wife died. God told Ezekiel not to show his grief so he would be an example of how stunned the people would be when Jerusalem would be destroyed by Babylon and their loved ones would die. When I was reading about Ezekiel's wife dying, I thought about my wife and how I would react if God was to ask me to do the same if she pre-deceased me. Just the thought of it caused me to cry a good portion of that night.

Yeshua's grieving was not limited to the loss of a loved one. He also grieved the separation from His heavenly Father and He grieved the thought of the loss of His own life. After His last Passover with His disciples, He knew He was going to be taken and turned over to the authorities to be falsely tried and then to be killed. He took His disciples to a garden area at the base of the Mount of Olives where an olive press was located, an area called Gethsemane, which is translated, the place of pressing.

Yeshua took His disciples to this place of pressing where self was going to be totally crushed out of Him. Knowing that in a few hours He was going to be betrayed by a friend, Judas, He asked His disciples to pray for Him and for themselves. Yeshua went off by Himself and prayed earnestly. The pressure of having the sins of the world placed upon Him was so intense that He experienced a rare medical condition called hematohidrosis. Under this extremely stressful experience His blood vessels ruptured, adding blood to His sweat.

Three different times Yeshua went back and forth between His private place to pray and His disciples. Each time He found that they had let Him down. They were not praying for Him, they had fallen back to sleep each time. Yeshua was facing death in just a few hours and He was all alone, no one helping or supporting Him.

But He was not totally alone. He went back to praying and was in the presence of His Father who had not left Him. Not yet anyway.

Each time during these three different prayer times Yeshua prayed for His Father to remove, if possible, "the cup" from Him. What was this cup? Yeshua had just finished a Passover seder with His disciples. During the Passover, four cups of wine (or grape juice) are drunk. Each cup has symbolism in relation to the exodus out of Egypt, Yeshua's life, and our lives. The names of the four cups are (there are some variations depending on various traditions): the cup of sanctification, the cup of salvation, the cup of judgment, and the cup of praise.

I think the cup that Yeshua had in mind was the cup of judgment. This cup originally symbolized the Red Sea closing on the Egyptian army that chased after God's people while the Red Sea was still parted. That event prefigured God's final judgment on those who will rebel against God's love and warnings. It is referred to as *"the wine of the wrath of God...the cup of His indignation"* (Revelation 14:10).

Why would Yeshua think that the wine of the wrath of God, the cup of His indignation, the cup of judgment would apply to Him? Because He was going to have the sins of the world placed upon Him and *"the wages of sin is death"* (Romans 6:23). It's not just an earthly death, but an eternal death, an eternal separation from heaven and the heavenly Father. The death that Yeshua experienced is referred to as the *"second death"* (Revelation 2:11; 20:6,14; 21:8). The first death is from our earthly life and the second is from our eternal life. This is what Yeshua was grieving as He sweat blood.

Yeshua did not end His prayers with a request to be spared the second death, the eternal death; rather He continued saying, *"Nevertheless, not what I will, but what You will"* (Mark 14:36). His earthly nature, that He had temporarily received while here on earth, did not want to die either death. In agonizing prayer self was crushed out and died as He surrendered all to the will of His heavenly Father. From that moment, Yeshua had peace and had courage to face the mob, the accusers, the authorities, the whip, the beatings, and the cross, and in the end pray, *"Father, forgive them for they do not know what they do"* (Luke 23:34).

You might be grieving, ahead of time, some possible future loss or the inevitable loss of your life here on this earth. I encourage you to surrender those fears to the Lord, even in agonizing prayer if necessary, and ask for the Lord's will to be done, not yours. Receive His peace by faith, knowing His will is always best.

While Yeshua was hanging on the cross, His heavenly Father needed to shield Himself from Yeshua so that the brightness of His glory did not destroy Yeshua as He bore the sins of the world. This caused tremendous grief to Yeshua as He cried out, quoting from David's Psalm 22:1, *"My God, My God, why have You forsaken Me?"* (Mark 15:34). It was very soon after that when His heart burst and He physically died.

Thankfully, His heavenly Father did not allow Yeshua to remain in the grave. Rather, on the third day from the Passover, the day during the Feast of Unleavened Bread when the firstfruits of the harvest were given to God, Yeshua was raised back to life. *"The gift of God is eternal life..."* (Romans 6:23).

While there may be times when we feel forsaken by God, we have a wonderful promise that says, *"I will never leave you nor forsake you"* (Hebrews 13:5). We are not called to bear the sins of the world. We are not even called to bear our own sins; Yeshua has already born them for us. In order for us to carry them we have to take them from Him, and why would we want to do that?

We started this chapter with Yeshua grieving the loss of John and we also read about Him grieving His forthcoming death and being separated from the One He loved the most. There is another time when He will grieve. Yeshua will grieve throughout eternity for those who refuse His invitations to heaven, those who refuse His substitution on their behalf as the sacrificial Lamb of God to take away our sins. Just the thought of His eternal heartache should cause us to share His love with everyone we meet before it is too late for them to receive it.

PAUSE, PONDER, AND PROCEED

1. Are you thankful to know that Yeshua experienced situational depression while He was here on earth living temporarily in the flesh (with emotions, feelings, and thoughts just as ours) and thus can relate to what you go through? If you have not let Him know how thankful you are for that lately, take a moment now and tell Him.

2. Did you think that being depressed was a sin? If so, are you relieved to know it is not?

3. While being depressed is not a sin, and while there are many factors that are not sinful that can lead to

depression, sin is one of the avoidable, unnecessary things that can lead to depression. Thus it is always good to be allowing the Holy Spirit to convict us if there is any known, conscious, rebelliously held-onto sin in our lives so that we can go to Yeshua to receive forgiveness and deliverance from the power and record of the sin. A good example of the type of continual prayer we should have to be in tune with the Holy Spirit's conviction would be David's prayer, *"Search me, O God, and know my heart; try me, and know my anxieties; and see if there is any wicked way in me, and lead me in the way everlasting"* (Psalm 139:23-24).

4. If you are grieving the loss of a loved one and have not taken the time to stop and remember the person and grieve your loss, I encourage you to carve out a time in your schedule and practice the principle of sitting *shiva* (even if it is not for a full seven days) as discussed in this chapter.

5. If you are grieving the loss of a loved one and have not yet thanked God for the time you had with your loved one, and the life God gave them, and to praise God for being God, I encourage you to do so now.

6. If you are grieving the loss of a loved one and have not yet experienced closure, consider doing something that will help you with that. It could be visiting the graveside and saying goodbye, or lighting a candle in remembrance of them, etc.

7. If you are grieving the loss of a loved one, ask your-self these three questions:

    a. What did you have from that relationship?

    b. What did you lose from their passing?

    c. What do you still have from that relationship that you can keep with you as you are now in the next chapter of your life?

8. If you have been hurt by someone's words or actions while you were mourning the loss of a loved one (or any type of loss), ask God to give you the ability to forgive them.

9. If you are struggling with trusting God with your future of some desire, plan, goal, pray Yeshua's prayer, *"Not what I will, but what You will."*

10. Are you thankful that Yeshua died the second death for you so that you never have to experience separation from God? If you have not thanked Him for that lately, pause now and do so.

11. Are there people you know who are grieving the loss of a loved one (or the loss of a position, or reputation, or ability) who God can use you to encourage? If so, why don't you put this book down and take time to let them know you love them?

12. Do you know someone who does not yet know the love of God? If God is bringing a specific person to your mind right now, I encourage you to put this book down and pray that God gives you the opportunity to show or tell them of His love for them.

13

JUDAS—DEMONIC POSSESSION

DEPRESSION IS NOT DEMON POSSESSION, BUT DEMON POSSES-sion can at times play a part in a person being depressed.

Judas is a sad story of what could have been. Judas was one of Yeshua's twelve disciples, even the treasurer of the group. But instead of being known as a help to Yeshua, he is referred to in infamy as *"Judas Iscariot, the son of Simon, for it was he who would betray Him"* (John 6:71).

The Scriptures tell us Judas became possessed by the devil. It specifically says, *"Then Satan entered Judas, surnamed Iscariot, who was numbered among the twelve"* (Luke 22:3).

Many people today, even some among Bible-reading people, don't believe there is a devil. Of those who do believe there is a devil, many have no idea of his influence or his methods. I think he prefers it that way.

The Bible is very clear, there is a devil. He was an important angel in heaven before he chose to sin and had to be cast out of heaven. He is such a cunning deceiver that he had one third of the angels following him (Revelation 12:4,9). Can you imagine that? One third of the angels who had not known sin, stood before God, lived in heaven, enjoyed the peace and bliss of God's goodness, were still deceived by this liar? If one third of the angels while still in heaven were able to be deceived how much more can we be?

We should not underestimate the devil's ability to trick us. He tricked Adam and Eve by getting them to believe God's word did not mean what He said it meant. He tricked them into thinking God was withholding something good from them. If you have ever been tempted to feel that way, I would like to remind you that *"God is love,"* that *"He does not change,"* and *"no good thing will He withhold from those who walk uprightly"* (1 John 4:8; Malachi 3:6; Psalm 84:11).

You may be asking, "If God is love, why did He allow there to be a devil?" That is a good question. The brief answer is, "Because He is love." Love allows free choice.

A stupid question is sometimes thrown out to taunt people who believe God is all powerful. It goes something like this, "If God is all powerful, can He make a rock that is so big He can't lift it?" A good response might be, "Yes, but He is not stupid enough to do so." But in many ways God has created a rock so big even He cannot lift it. That rock is free choice. God could have blocked Eve

174

and Adam from eating the fruit from the tree of the knowledge of good and evil, but He did not take away the wonderful gift of free choice that He has given to humanity.

Because God technically could have blocked Eve and Adam, He at times takes the blame for the suffering that takes place on this earth. But if He did take away our free choice, even sometimes, we would not be humans we would be robots. Robots do not have the capacity to love. In order to be able to truly love, we need to have the freedom to be able to choose not to love. God wants us to freely choose to love Him, because that is the only type of real love there is.

To be true to Himself and to truly, equally love everyone, God has had to grant this unliftable rock of free choice not only to you and me, but to even the hitlers of this world (lowercase used on purpose). Fortunately, we are only passing through this earth. This troubled world is not our home, we are on our way to heaven where no one will ever choose to rebel against God again.

God gives us free choice and He allowed free choice among His angels in heaven. One of those angels was called lucifer. He was highly privileged and was called a *"covering cherub"* (Ezekiel 28:16), indicating he might have been one of two that stood next to God's throne. The sanctuary, that God instructed Moses to build, had two golden angels representing those two special angels in heaven. In the sanctuary Moses built, the golden angels covered the mercy seat of the Ark of the Covenant, which held the Ten Commandments. The Scriptures describe lucifer as being created perfect (Ezekiel 28:15), yet one who chose to become proud and then fell. When he fell he became known as satan or the devil.

God had to cast lucifer out of heaven, but before He did, lucifer gained the following of one third of the angels. Lucifer's argument was that God was wrong and he, lucifer, could do a better job of running things. If God would have destroyed lucifer at that point, many more angels might have believed lucifer's lies. How can God get the message out there that He is The Good One while satan is constantly tempting people to abuse the magnificent gift of free choice that God has granted to us?

Here is an illustration to help you understand God's predicament. Let's imagine you are at work and one of your coworkers, named Lucy, accuses you of stealing from the company. What would people think if you went and killed that coworker? They would think you were trying to cover up the evidence, that you killed Lucy to stop her from testifying against you. You would not only be deemed a thief, but a murderer as well.

So what you might do is hire a detective to set up some hidden cameras to determine who really is stealing from the company. Let's imagine the cameras pick up Lucy stealing from the company. You would now have the evidence you need to clear your name and to convict the wrongdoer. God is using the events on this small planet to demonstrate to the universe that lucifer is a liar and that God is just and good and love.

In a sense, we are the evidence that lucifer's lies are just that, nothing but lies. We are the proof to the universe that lucifer's ways lead to sadness and destruction and that God is powerful enough to set us free from satan's hold. We are living proof that God's ways bring about joy, peace, happiness, love, forgiveness, redemption, hope, trust, and abundant life. We are the evidence that God and satan are fighting for; by our choices we get to help tip the balances in God's favor. When all the world has seen and heard enough to make their choices, then God can rid the universe of satan once and for all.

After everyone has seen for themselves the horrible results of choosing sin over God, the Bible promises us that, *"Affliction shall not rise up the second time"* (Nahum 1:9). These horrendous few thousands of years of earth's history will stand as a testimony for all eternity and no one—human, angel, or any other created being—will ever choose sin over God again. The new heaven and new earth will be nothing but joyful happiness, filled with full true love for God and for one another. As the wonderful song "Amazing Grace" says, "When we've been there ten thousand years bright shining as the sun, we'll have no less days to sing God's praise than when we first begun." If it will take a few thousand atrocious years to prove to the universe for all eternity that God truly is love, then we will proclaim, "It was worth it."

It is satan who brings hardships into our lives. Then he tempts us to blame God for the sufferings. In the book of Job, recorded in the Bible, Job is described as righteous and prosperous. Then satan came before God boasting that he rules over all the earth. God pointed to Job and reminded satan there was at least one whom he did not rule over. But satan accused Job of serving God for selfish purposes only, because Job was prospering. He insinuated that if God took Job's prosperity away, Job would curse God. To prove satan wrong God allowed him to do to Job whatever he chose as long as he did not touch Job. Notice that God did not do it, but he permitted satan to do what he wanted. That would make evident both satan's and Job's characters. Then satan caused Job one disaster after another. Within hours, Job lost all his wealth, property, and even children. In all of that loss, Job testified that God is good, stating *"The Lord gave, and the Lord has taken away; blessed be the name of the Lord"* (Job 1:21).

More furious than before, satan taunted God that the only reason Job still loved Him was because God had not let him afflict Job bodily. God again allowed satan to do whatever he wanted to Job, except taking his life. So satan caused a horrible, painful, illness to afflict Job. But even in all that Job did not sin. In the end, Job remained faithful and God again blessed Job with prosperity.

A similar story is playing out today in your life and mine. It is playing out before the entire universe. God is proving to all the universe there are people who will trust Him no matter what satan throws at us. God is allowing the "evidence" to build a full case against satan and for us. Certainly before the unfallen angels would be comfortable with having us live for eternity with them, they would have a right to an assurance that we would not ruin heaven and make it like earth. They deserve the proof that no matter how we are harassed, persecuted, or tempted, nothing will move us from our loyalty to God.

In a nutshell, some of the reasons God allows us to experience suffering for the relatively short time we live on earth are: freedom of choice; a demonstration to the universe; proving satan a liar; proving God as just and good; and a test of our loyalty. There is much more to it than just that, but hopefully that clarifies a little bit of God's predicament as He faces satan's accusations.

While that might make a lot of sense, logic is not enough to make us feel better when we are going through difficulties and hardships. It takes a choice on our part to allow that logic to point our hearts to God, trusting Him to heal us of our pain. This includes both the pain we suffer as a result of other people's misuse of their free choice, and the pain we have caused due to our poor choices.

I invite you to pause the reading right here and to make the choice right now, in spite of your problems, to ask God to fill you with faith in His love for you.

In the end this will all work out for our good so that we also will have the assurance nothing will be allowed into heaven that will cause another fall. After this sad experience and trial is complete here on this old earth, there will never be suffering of any type ever again.

So how does satan work in relation to our lives today? What does the Bible mean when it says, *"Satan entered Judas"* in Luke 22:3)?

I will describe four different ways satan works in relation to us—some others may describe more ways or less ways or identify them differently and that is fine, but the generally agreed upon point is that satan works in various ways and to varying degrees in order to cause us to fall. The four descriptions I use are referred to as harassment, temptation, control, and possession. (I might have obtained those titles from someone else, but I cannot remember from whom.)

We have just looked at a biblical example of *harassment* in the life of Job. The devil harasses all of us. This world is in a fallen state and bad things happen. There are and will be problems. Financial problems, weather-related problems, health problems, interpersonal problems, things break, things don't go as planned, situations don't work out as hoped. Some of these are results of bad choices we or others have made, some of these are just a result of living in a sinful world, some things just happen, and some of these are a result of evil angels (demons) causing bad things to happen. No matter what reason they happen, we again have the promises and assurances from God that He will never leave us or forsake us, that He will work all things out together for good, and that we can be more than conquerors through Him (Hebrews 13:5; Romans 8:28; 31-39).

Regarding the second way satan works, Eve and even Yeshua are examples of being *tempted.* All of us are tempted to do wrong. Satan whispers an insinuation into our minds, usually using our "voice" so it sounds like we are thinking it. This is unfortunately "normal" for life on this earth. We are all tempted. The temptation is not sin; it is just satan's lie. If we believe the lie and act upon the wrong, it becomes sin. As Yeshua demonstrated, even though we "hear" the temptation, we don't have to yield to the devil and sin. It is possible by trusting in God's strength to *"submit to God. Resist the devil and he will flee from us"* (James 4:7). The Complete Jewish Bible states it this way: *"Therefore, submit to God. Moreover, take a stand against the Adversary, and he will flee from you."*

There is a very real battle that takes place. It has been depicted as an angel on each shoulder, one good, one bad, both whispering into our ears. One whispers temptations, doubts, frustrations, fears, lies, reasons to be bitter, angry, jealous, impatient, selfish, or prideful. The other angel is whispering hope, faith, God's promises, love, truth, logic, warnings, and encouragements to not act upon those temptations nor to think or do evil.

Here is an example of the battle that goes on in our minds—not necessarily an example of temptation or sin, but the principle is the same:

"I should put my seat belt on."

"I don't feel like it."

"I could get a ticket."

"What are the chances of that?"

"I could get into an accident."

"I'm not going that far."

"You never know."

"It restricts me. I don't like it. I'll put it on when the A/C kicks in and the car cools down a bit."

"It is a bad habit. I'm being lazy, just put it on, it's a good example for the kids. I'll be safer. If I form the habit of doing what is right, it will be easier to do what is right more often. If I resist by being lazy in this easy chore, it will be easier to resist in other areas as well."

The two voices battle it out; the final choice we make is up to us.

Each one is tempted when he is drawn away by his own desires and enticed. Then, when desire has conceived, it gives birth to sin; and sin, when it is full-grown, brings forth death (James 1:14-15).

No temptation has overtaken you except such as is common to man; but God is faithful, who will not allow you to be tempted beyond what you are able, but with the temptation will also make the way of escape, that you may be able to bear it (1 Corinthians 10:13).

...I write to you, so that you may not sin... (1 John 2:1).

A third way the devil works is by *controlling* us. This is beyond temptation but not quite possession. A biblical example of this is when Yeshua took His disciples to Caesarea Philippi and asked them who they thought He was. Peter responded, *"You are the Messiah, Son of the living God"* (Matthew 16:16 TLV). Yeshua told him that he was correct, and that this was not revealed to him by man, but by God Himself. That is quite a compliment to Peter, that God was revealing things to him.

Just a few verses later, Yeshua told His disciples that he would *"be killed, and raised the third day"* (Matthew 16:21). Peter responded again, this time saying, *"this shall not happen to You!"* (Matthew 16:22). Instead of being complimented for his comment, Yeshua said to Peter, *"Get behind Me, Satan! You are an offense to Me, for you are not mindful of the things of God, but the things of men"* (Matthew 16:23). Wow.

Note that the text says that Yeshua said to Peter, *"Get behind Me, Satan."* He said it to Peter, but He was speaking to satan. Moments before Yeshua had said that God was speaking to Peter; then satan was speaking through Peter. How can that be? Peter had an incomplete and imperfect understanding of the Lord's plan. In the area of who the Messiah was, Peter was listening to God. In the area of what Messiah's role or purpose was, Peter had his own ideas, which reflected what most people at that time thought. In that area of Peter's life he was not only willing to believe satan's lie, but he allowed his mouth to be used by satan. In this way, satan was attempting to confuse the disciples and even discourage Yeshua from drinking the cup He was to drink. That area of Peter's life was under the control of satan and needed not only a gentle correction, but a firm rebuke from the Lord against satan.

We may not have a complete understanding of satan's battle tactics, but it seems at times that he is able to gain a fuller control over certain areas of our lives. This might explain why some habits for some people are harder to break than others. One person might have found breaking the habit of smoking was easy while breaking the habit of alcohol was difficult. For someone else it might be the exact opposite. The same could be true for the habit of negativity or gossip or any habit. Possibly the more we yield to satan in a certain area, the more control he has over that area.

There could also be an opening for control over certain areas of our lives because of yielding to satan in those areas by our parents, grandparents, or great-grandparents. The Bible says the effects of wrong choices can pass to the third and fourth generations (Exodus 20:5).

The difference between temptation and control would be that temptation comes as satan tries to convince us to think or do something that is not in harmony with God's word. Control might be described as a compulsion to do or think what is against God's word. Temptation can be overcome by a choice, while control needs to be overcome by an intentional drawing near to God and a purposeful, willful resisting by the power of God and prayer.

Again, this is a general illustration of some of satan's strategies. We humans are very complex, and we are dealing with a devil who is very intelligent, crafty, and who has myriads of evil angels working with him. Thus, the potential scenarios depicting the battle taking place in our lives are innumerable. Words are often insufficient to describe the reality we experience and see around us. The point I am trying to make is that there seem to be degrees of influence that satan has over us—yet always remember that God is more than a match for anything satan throws at us.

The fourth way, in this list, where the Bible describes satan's work against us is referred to as *possession*. We have already seen that satan was able to enter Judas. The Gospels and the book of Acts describe several accounts of people being possessed. Sometimes these people are totally out of their minds, other times they are functioning quite well as in the case with Judas.

It seems that possession is the total control by the devil of a certain area of our lives. We might be fine in every other area, but this one area, or several, is in the possession of the devil. That area or areas we have no control over whatsoever, he totally manipulates us in that area.

The devil does not always cause one who is possessed to look bad or even appear to be against God. The other disciples could not tell that Judas was possessed. Another example is in the book of Acts. A woman who sold idols was following Paul saying, *"These men are servants of El Elyon* [Most High God], *who are proclaiming to you the way of salvation."* It seems that Paul did not discern the extent of satan's influence in her life right away, since it continued for several days. Eventually Paul said to the spirit (which was referred to as a spirit of divination), *"'I command you in the name of Messiah Yeshua to come out of her!' And it came out of her that very moment"* (Acts 16:17-18 TLV).

There are several things we can learn from this account and others like it. The spirit or demon had a specific job assignment, in this case, divination. Thus, a person can be possessed by several or even many different demons, each one having possession of a different area of the person's life. She was functioning and even looking like a follower of the way of salvation. The demon was in her and needed to be cast out. The demon was cast out by the power and the name of Yeshua the Messiah.

When a demon is inside a person, the demon has the ability to manipulate that area of the person's life. I think this analogy will be very helpful in understanding demon possession: demon possession is like when we have the flu. A virus enters us causing our nose to run, our eyes to tear, our throat to be sore, it causes us to sneeze, and other symptoms. We are not bad because we have the flu. We are not choosing to have a runny nose, but we can't help it. The virus might have entered through wrong choices we made such as going out on a cold day with wet hair and no jacket or wrong choices someone else made (they had a cold and did not wash their hands, etc.).

We are not good or bad because we have the flu. We just have the flu, that is all. The flu virus is not us, it is a separate living organism that has been able to inhabit us. When the virus is killed, the symptoms leave. That accurately describes what it is like to have a demon inside us. People who are possessed by at least one demon are not bad because they have a demon that "entered into" them. They are like people with a flu virus living in them, they are people with a demon living in them. Just as a virus can be overcome and leave, the demon can be forced to leave. When the flu leaves, the symptoms leave; when the demon leaves, satan's control of that area ends.

How does a demon enter into us? It seems there is more than one way. One possibility is through continuous, intentional wrong choices. People can be tempted and yield to that temptation repeatedly until they become controlled by it. If they resist the power of the Lord to break the control, that area could become possessed by the demon.

Another way seems to be hereditary. It is possible for a demon to transfer from a parent to the child. That, of course, doesn't seem fair, but who says the devil plays fair. Why to some children and not to all the children, why sometimes and not all the times, I don't know. And I don't care. What I do care about is getting rid of the demon. It is not as important to try to figure out everything the devil does as it is to know how God defeats the devil. When we have the flu, it is not as important to know why some people in the room caught the flu and others did not; the important thing is to kill the virus.

Another way seems to be when a person's will is broken, such as through rape, beatings, or other abuse. This, again, is not fair, but it seems to be the case. Why it is not in every single case of rape or abuse, I don't know. Again, the important thing is to get rid of the demon.

Some people think it is impossible for a believer to be possessed by the devil. That would seem like the ultimate deception to me. If we believe we are saved then we won't believe it is possible for satan to possess us and thus he can lurk unnoticed in a single area of our life. Or, on the other hand, we can sense we are possessed and then become discouraged, thinking we are not saved. But in actuality, God works in our lives step by step. The day we come to Him He does not reveal every area of our lives that need victory. Throughout our lives, He works gradually, freeing us more and more from the devil's temptations, controls, and possessions.

Salvation has two main aspects to it, justification and sanctification.

- God saves us from the punishment of sin—giving us eternal life over death (justification). And God saves us from the power of sin—victory over temptation (sanctification).

- We are saved from the punishment of sin because of the Messiah's death for us (justification). We are saved from the power of sin because of the Messiah's life in us (sanctification).

- We can have salvation over death because of the Messiah's death (justification), while at the same time gaining salvation over temptations that face us day by day (sanctification).

- God's salvation in our lives over death (justification) is something that God accomplished on our behalf before we were born and without our permission. It is experienced and received by us by faith in His sacrificial death for us. In contrast, God's salvation over temptation (sanctification) is God's work on our behalf now with our permission and is received by faith in His power.

These two aspects of salvation work together, transforming us and preparing us for heaven. For that reason, it is possible to believe by faith in the sacrifice of the Messiah and be saved from the punishment of sin and yet at the same time still be dealing with demons that might have entered us before we were believers or that were forced upon us through abuse after we became believers. We will not be accountable in the judgment for unconscious ignorance.

Again, like the flu, having a demon in us does not make us good or bad. But when it is revealed to us, through conviction of the Holy Spirit, that we are being tempted or controlled or possessed by the devil, we have a choice whether or not we are going to call on the Lord to save us from it. We will be accountable for those conscious, willful choices.

Now to the important part, how do we get rid of the "virus," the demons? I don't know of an example in the Bible of someone having demons cast out of them without the intercession of others, but it might be possible. In all the Bible examples, someone else is praying and interceding on behalf of the person who is afflicted with a demon or demons. It is not the intercessor who is doing the casting out; it is the Lord God Almighty who does it. That is very important to remember. It is the Lord, responding to the prayer of a humble supplicant dependently crying out in faith in the power of the name of the Lord on behalf of someone else, that delivers the person.

When interceding on behalf of someone else, it is powerful to quote the Bible. The devil hates when we quote the Bible, claiming God's promises. That is one of the methods Yeshua used when He was tempted by the devil in the wilderness.

Singing sacred songs is powerful as well. Paul and Silas did this when they were locked up in a dungeon.

I don't recommend getting into conversations with the demons. But it can be helpful to call out the sin by name so it is exposed and can be confessed and forsaken. I don't recommend getting into an argument with demons, who sometimes speak out through the person who is being prayed for. Just continue to tell them that in the name, power, and authority of Yeshua the Messiah, because of His death and His resurrection, they have no right to remain in this person any longer. They must leave, not to transfer to anyone else, not to hide or divide, but to be bound up and reserved for judgment where they will be burned up and become ashes under the soles of our feet (see 2 Peter 2:4; Malachi 4:3; Ezekiel 28:18).

It does not have to be those exact words. I am not suggesting a formula or mere wording that works, but the truths of those words. The important principles are that it is the authority of the Messiah (not me or anyone else) that has power over the demons, and that it is because of His death and resurrection that the demons must obey.

In the book of Acts, the seven sons of Sceva tried to cast out a demon using the formula of calling on the name of the Lord, but not with humble, surrendered hearts:

> *But the evil spirit answered them, "I know Yeshua and I know about Paul, but who are you?" Then the man with the evil spirit sprang at them, subduing and overpowering all of them, so that they fled out of that house naked and wounded* (Acts 19:15-16 TLV).

More important than the right wording is having the right heart. Right hearts are those that are humble before God and submitted to Him, while at the same time filled with His Spirit, making them bold in the Lord. That is biblical meekness.

Make sure that whoever is doing the intercessory praying has and is allowing God to search their heart for any sins. If any sins are revealed, they must be confessed and forsaken by the power of the Lord. The person must be receiving the forgiveness of the Lord because of the Messiah's death on his behalf, and he needs to be accepting the gift of the Holy Spirit to fill him with God's character.

The same is true for the person being prayed for. His heart must be prepared in a similar manner. Don't rush into praying for someone or being prayed for unless all the parties are spiritually ready for it.

I strongly recommend that there is always more than one person doing the praying for someone else. One person can be doing most of the praying, speaking, quoting the Bible, and commanding in the name and authority of the Lord. The others can mostly be praying silently. There needs to be harmony and unity among those who are praying, or the demons will divide and conquer.

There needs to be one person leading out in the prayer session while the others are supporting him/her. The others, when invited by the leader, can also pray, quote Scripture, etc., but there still needs to be only one person leading each prayer session.

I went with a friend to visit a mutual friend who was in the hospital. We were not going there to pray for any demons to be cast out; it was just to be a friendly hospital visit. The man in the hospital was in my opinion a godly, saved person. I don't know if someone has a demon or not, but this man certainly had many issues. He had been badly abused as a child and struggled with several things in his life. He had had dozens of operations performed on him. He was in and out of the hospital for various issues, many of which never seemed to have a cause or a cure, yet the problems would come and go. While we were there, the hospitalized person started to speak with self-pity. "No one has it as bad as me," etc.

When he started to retell the story of his wife dying, the person who was with me got very angry and said, "You think you are the only one who has had problems, my wife died of cancer..."

The argument got so heated and loud that a nurse ran in from the hall and broke it up. The man in the hospital was eventually discharged and continued to struggle, but with gradual victories. However, the person who came with me was never the same soon after that. He could no longer hold down his job, he stopped attending services, he ended up on many prescribed medications, which have largely left him much different from who he once was. Again, I can't tell if someone is demon possessed or not (important point), but the timing of the change seemed very suspicious.

Demons are not to be messed with without putting on the armor of God. I don't believe the demons transfer from casual contact with someone who is demon possessed. If any demon or demons entered the friend who visited the hospital, it was because he opened himself up to it, not because he was visiting someone who had a demon or demons in him.

Demons have no choice; they must leave the person when the person is surrendering that area of their life to the Lord and when humble, surrendered intercessors are dependently calling on the name of the Lord for deliverance. Yet, they don't leave willingly or easily. Yeshua said it takes fasting and prayer. Obviously this means more than skipping a meal and praying, "Our Father..." It means both the person in need of help and the intercessors fasting from sin, turning from sin, setting aside time and having a clear mind (possibly by skipping meals or other activities), and denying themselves of carnal and natural lusts or cravings, while seeking the Lord earnestly and dependently for help and deliverance.

A person can be possessed by more than one demon; thus it could take several prayer sessions for the full deliverance to take place. But victory is assured in the power of Yeshua the Messiah.

It is vitally important when a demon is cast out, that the person be filled with the Holy Spirit. Yeshua told a parable of a house that was swept clean of a demon, but the house was not filled up, it was left empty; so, the demon came back and this time with seven other demons even more wicked than the first (Matthew 12:44-45).

We can see that before, during, and after God casts out the demons we need to be seeking Him continually, humbly, and fervently. Seeking Him with all our hearts, all our souls, and with all our might. That includes praying continually, reading God's Word daily, and attending services regularly. That means: dying to self daily; confessing our need of Him; giving God permission to search us and show us the next area He wants to give us victory over; accepting the Messiah's death for forgiveness and cleansing; accepting the power of the Holy Spirit for change and renewal; and moving out in faith and in the power of the Lord to gain continual victories.

How did it end for Judas? Both Judas and Peter denied and betrayed Yeshua in His final hours on earth. Peter went out with much weeping and re-surrendered his life to the Lord, confessing his sin and receiving God's forgiveness and power to have victory in the future. Judas could have had the same forgiveness, the same deliverance, yet instead he chose to take his own life, hanging himself. A very sad ending to such potential. That does not have to be our end. We can overcome by the power of the Lord God Almighty. His arms are open to save no matter how bad our past has been. He has a glorious future for all of us if we will just accept it by faith. And if we lack faith? Cry out to Him to give it and He will do so.

Peter, like David, was not perfect, but both were willing to accept rebuke. That made the difference between Peter and Judas, and between David and Saul. It often makes all the difference in the world. The Lord says:

> *As many as I love, I rebuke and chasten. Therefore be zealous and repent. Behold, I stand at the door and knock. If anyone hears My voice and opens the door, I will come in to him and dine with him, and he with Me. To him who overcomes I will grant to sit with Me on My throne, as I also overcame and sat down with My Father on His throne* (Revelation 3:19-21).

> *Let the righteous strike me; it shall be a kindness. And let him rebuke me; it shall be as excellent oil; let my head not refuse it...* (Psalm 141:5).

Mentioning Peter, it is interesting to see a couple of the things that might have kept him from hanging himself after he denied the Lord. During Yeshua's last Passover with His disciples, Yeshua warned Peter that he would deny Him three times. Just hours later, Peter snuck into the courtyard at Yeshua's trial and stood by a fire to warm himself. Three different times people asked him if he was a disciple of Yeshua, and three times he denied Him, just as Yeshua prophesied. Peter went out and wept bitterly, but he did not give up. Three days later he was with the other disciples. Mary Magdalene went to the tomb and the Bible says Yeshua *"appeared first to Mary Magdalene, out of whom He had cast seven demons. 'Go, tell His disciples—and Peter—that He is going before you into Galilee'"* (Mark

16:9,7). Yeshua sent a message specifically mentioning that Peter was still accepted. What love. The Bible is clear, you and I, regardless of our mistakes, are just as accepted by the Lord as was Peter.

Then a few days after Yeshua's resurrection, Yeshua met His disciples on the shores of the Sea of Galilee by an open fire. Yeshua asked Peter if he loved Him three different times. It was by a fire at dawn that Peter denied the Lord three times, and now he confessed the Lord three times at dawn by a fire. Sometimes God replaces a bad memory with a good memory. After Peter's denial, fires might have reminded him of those denials; now instead of reminding him of his denials, a fire reminded him of his commitment to love the Lord and to feed His sheep.

I was on the shores of the Sea of Galilee telling this very story to a group during one of our tours to the Holy Land when a lady named Donna asked if she could give a testimony. Donna's grandson had been swept away and drowned a few years prior while he was driving his street cleaning truck across a flood-swollen bridge. Donna told us how that morning, as we were on our way to the site where Yeshua asked Peter if he loved Him, she saw a street cleaning truck for the first time since her grandson's death, and how the sad memory of her grandson's death was now replaced with the site of the Sea of Galilee and the story of God's love for Peter and for all of us. Sometimes we need to face our bad memories and let God replace them with good ones.

Again, depression is not demon possession, but demon possession could be a factor in depression. If you are struggling with depression, I would suggest that you consider demon possession as the last possible cause. Before considering demon possession as a possible cause, first implement all of the various helpful tips in this book, plus implement the NEWSTART program mentioned in the chapter titled Elijah—Highs and Lows, and attend Weimar Institute's Depression Recovery program.

PAUSE, PONDER, AND PROCEED

1. Do you now have a better understanding of why God did not destroy lucifer from the start?

2. Do you now better understand how the wonderful gift of free choice has also been the reason why there is suffering in the world?

3. Have you had a hard time receiving correction? True humility and the ability to receive rebuke is a gift from God, it does not come naturally. Choose to surrender to God and let Him give you the mind of Yeshua. *"Humble yourselves in the sight of the Lord, and He will lift you up"* (James 4:10).

4. Satan caused Job to lose all his children and many possessions; but even though Job did not realize it was satan who was the cause of those problems, he still chose to trust that God was good, loving, and knew what was best. If you have been tempted to blame God or be angry at God for any suffering you have experienced, are you willing now to say by faith, as Job did, *"The Lord gave and the Lord has taken away, blessed be the name of the Lord."*

5. Do you appreciate that God has entrusted to you the powerful freedom of choice, and is allowing you to

demonstrate to the universe that satan is a liar, and that God is just and good?

6. Do you want to allow the Holy Spirit to fill you with grace so that you will pass the test of your loyalty to God now and forever and for Him to give you the power to always choose God over willful sin?

7. Is there some area of your life in which you have not been able to gain the victory, no matter how many times you have prayed, confessed, and sought the Lord about it? Maybe a demon is possessing that area of your life. If so, continue in prayer, continue to surrender that area of your life. Ask God if there is something about that sin that needs to be confessed, or if there is someone you need to forgive. Ask God to give you the ability to forgive that person, persons, or yourself. Seek out godly friends who are covered in the armor of God, who understand the battle between God and satan, who know how to dependently call on the power of the name of the Lord, and ask them to intercede on your behalf and to pray with you for deliverance.

JOSEPH—NOT DEPRESSED

JOSEPH DOES NOT ACTUALLY FIT THE TITLE OF THIS BOOK, *Depressed People of the Bible.* To human reasoning it seems he had every justifiable reason to be depressed. He had several depression hits, but we have no record of him being depressed and we have recorded history from his childhood to his death.

Joseph lost his mother when he was young and he was hated and abused by his brothers. Then, when he was still young, he was separated from his father, his home, and everything he knew, being sold into slavery. After a few years of slavery, he was falsely accused of a crime he did not commit and put in prison for several years. While in prison, Joseph helped pharaoh's cupbearer, who promised to remember Joseph and help him, but he did not. Even after Joseph got out of prison and was put in a very responsible position with great wealth, power, fame, and influence, with a wife and two sons, he still had to eat his meals alone (at least at work).

Talk about a life filled with grief, sorrow, loss, hardship, disappointments, rejection, oppression, and loneliness. How many depression hits can you count in his life? Yet there is no record of him being depressed, although he, no doubt, had times of great sadness and grief. Despite his great hardships, the record seems to indicate he did not let depression overtake him. How do we know he did not let depression overtake him? And how did he do it?

Before we answer those questions let's look at a few things in Joseph's life and then ask another question. When Joseph was serving as a slave, his master put him in charge of all his household. When he was in prison, the one in charge of the prison put him in charge of all the prisoners. When Joseph appeared before pharaoh, the pharaoh said, "Can we find anyone as this, a man in whom is the Spirit of God?" and he put him in charge of all of Egypt.

If Joseph had been sitting around in the slave house crying and weeping day and night for weeks on end because of his difficulties, would his master have put him in charge of his whole house? If Joseph had been sitting around in the prison complaining over and over again how life was not fair, how he didn't deserve this treatment, how it was all his master's wife's fault, that the food was horrible, that he did not get a fair trial, that the cupbearer reneged on his promise, and don't forget his brothers—those no-good-niks—would the one in charge of the prison have trusted Joseph to be in charge of all the prisoners? If for twenty years Joseph had remained bitter and angry at all those who wronged him and had not forgiven them, would the pharaoh have seen the Spirit of God in him and make him the second most influential person in Egypt? I think not.

When we hold on to feelings of unfairness, even when things really aren't fair, like in Joseph's case, rehashing the bad things that have happened to us over and over again, and hold on to bitterness and resentment, it will show on our faces. It will eat up our hearts. It will affect our mental and emotional health.

So how is it that Joseph did not give in to the temptation to be overcome with sadness and complain nonstop? How was he able to forgive instead of holding on to anger and bitterness? What he said to his brothers must have been going through his head for twenty years, *"You meant it for evil against me, but God meant it for good... to save many people alive"* (Genesis 50:20).

Joseph kept choosing to believe that and saying that to himself when he was in the pit that his brother's threw him into, in the slave room he was confined to, and the prison cell he was locked up in. Those were Joseph's physical and emotional "caves." He overcame those caves by saying to himself, "Even if they meant it for evil, God will turn it out for good to save many people." That is just as true for our experiences as well.

In spite of what evil people do to us, or the bad things that happen to us, or the mistakes we make ourselves, *"We know that all things work together for good to those who love God, to those who are called according to His purpose"* (Romans 8:28). If we focus on that, it is hard to be down for too long.

As I heard one person put it, "Unforgiveness is a poison pill that someone eats hoping it will kill someone else." Unforgiveness often does not affect the people who wrong us. Sometimes they don't even know we exist. Yet it will eat us from the inside out if we hold on to it. Joseph chose to forgive his brothers and chose to believe God had a plan. As a result, other people saw God's Spirit in him.

So how did Joseph forgive his brothers and others who treated him so poorly? For the answer to that question reread the section about true forgiveness in the chapter about Jonah("Jonah—A Classic Example"). What Jonah did wrong regarding forgiveness, Joseph did right.

If you are going through hell, don't stop! Keep going right on through until you get to the other side. Too often when we are going through hell we stop, sit down, and get discouraged. Then not only are we in hell (figuratively), but we get burned while we are there. Instead, be like the guy walking across hot coals—don't stop. Keep your eyes focused on God's goal set before you. Keep your eyes on heaven. Look to your reward.

God has only good planned for us. That "good" might include being hated by our siblings, threatened with murder, sold into slavery, falsely imprisoned, forgotten, and then be made the second most influential person in one of the most powerful countries in the world and be instrumental in saving many lives. Or His "good" for you might not be quite as dramatic as that. Whatever plan He has for you trust that *"no good thing will He withhold from them who walk uprightly"* (Psalm 84:11). Whatever the path He appoints us, heaven is the end goal for us and for those He wants to use us to influence. If getting there must take us through thorns or thrones, so be it. It is not the journey that counts but the destination.

We will be fulfilling God's plan for our lives if, by God's power, we let go of the past and do all that we can do in our present situation for the salvation of souls for His kingdom.

A young teenage woman was depressed and suicidal. After years of dealing with sexual, physical, and emotional abuse by family and others, Valerie (not her real name) was discouraged and felt worthless. The feelings of worthlessness were compounded by the fact that much of this mistreatment was perpetrated by those professing to be following God. She believed she had to endure abuse because it was a sin to refuse. Despite what she had been through, she never felt that she had really suffered enough, since she believed she must deserve abuse and mistreatment for being a sinner. She had hoped God would make up for some of that by allowing her to marry the man she wanted more than anything else. When he fell in love with someone else, she was heartbroken and felt even more worthless than she did before.

In the depths of her shame and feelings of worthlessness, she misguidedly thought she could release herself from her own sense of guilt. Valerie felt that her life was a waste. She thought if she harmed herself enough to achieve whatever level of punishment she deserved, she wouldn't feel as guilty for living unpunished anymore. Valerie began cutting herself. Yet no matter how much abuse she accepted from others or how much she hurt herself, she never felt like she was punished sufficiently to accept anything good in life.

Then she read the chapter about Joseph in the book *Jewish Discoveries* (also written by this author). Valerie read how God gave Joseph the ability to forgive. She also learned that forgiveness was not the same as accepting abuse and enduring it. She learned she can be merciful and forgiving to others while also recognizing she should be treated respectfully. Valerie realized that cutting herself was an effort to atone for herself.

As she continued to read, she came to accept that the Messiah had already atoned for her through His own suffering. She didn't need to shed her blood since He already gave His for her. Valerie concluded that to harm herself because she didn't feel good enough was to tell God the Messiah's blood isn't good enough, that her blood can do it better. Of course that is not true. There is nothing we can do to atone for our sins or the sins of others. There is nothing we can do to make God love or accept us more. He has already paid the ultimate price, He already loves us with infinite love.

Valerie still has dark times, but she knows that in the midst of it God is holding her. She now knows she does not have to feel hopeless no matter what happens because like Job she can say:

> As for me, I know that my Redeemer lives, and he will stand upon the earth at last. And after my body has decayed, yet in my body I will see God! I will see him for myself. Yes, I will see him with my own eyes. I am overwhelmed at the thought! (Job 19:25-27 New Living Translation)

Valerie used to worry a lot about God making decisions that would hurt her, but now she knows what God says is true: "'I know the plans that I have for you,' says the Lord. 'They are plans for good and not for disaster, to give you a future and a hope'" (Jeremiah 29:11 New Living Translation).

It has been more than ten years since Valerie has cut or abused herself. She believes her negative experiences led her to have more hope than she would have otherwise. Today Valerie is very active in helping others to know God and to understand His Word, the Bible.

No matter what you have been through, even if it is as bad as what Joseph or Valerie have been through, God has a great plan for you: *"Trust in the Lord with all your heart, and lean not on your own understanding; in all your ways acknowledge Him, and He shall direct your paths"* (Proverbs 3:5-6).

PAUSE, PONDER, AND PROCEED

1. If you have been rehashing over and over again in your mind or with your mouth some wrong that someone has done to you, and you are now willing to let God stop that pattern, ask God to bring every thought into captivity to the obedience of Messiah, and say with Joseph, "They meant it for evil against me, but God meant it for good...to save many people alive." Continue to say that and believe it every time those past wrongs against you try to obsess your mind.

2. If you have been swallowing the poison pill of unforgiveness, hoping it will hurt the offender, choose to surrender that to Yeshua. Let Him deal with them. *"Beloved, do not avenge yourselves, but rather give place to wrath; for it is written, 'Vengeance is Mine, I will repay,' says the Lord"* (Romans 12:19).

3. If you are going through figurative hell, what is the goal ahead? What can you be doing to make it

through? *"Whatever things are true, whatever things are noble, whatever things are just, whatever things are pure, whatever things are lovely, whatever things are of good report, if there is any virtue and if there is anything praiseworthy—meditate on these things"* (Philippians 4:8).

4. If you have been cutting yourself or abusing yourself in any way—*"present your bodies a living sacrifice, holy, acceptable to God, which is your reasonable service. And do not be conformed to this world, but be transformed by the renewing of your mind, that you may prove what is that good and acceptable and perfect will of God"* (Romans 12:1-2).

15

CONCLUSION

SOME THINGS WE CAN LEARN FROM THESE EXPERIENCES are: Many godly people experience depression. It is not a sin to be depressed. God has ways out of depression.

There can be many causes of depression that are not covered in this book. If you are still struggling with bouts of depression, do not be discouraged. This book is not intended for the diagnosis or treatment of depression.

There is still hope. Clinical depression does not come on overnight (although at times it might look like it did); similarly it may take some time for the changes you need to implement in your life to take place and for your body to start feeling the positive effects from those changes.

Continue to implement the Bible principles brought out in this book and feel free to contact the professionals at Weimar Institute in Weimar, California who will be able to give you a thorough evaluation and help you see how many depression hits can be reversed in your life.

I hope you were encouraged in reading the experiences of some of the people mentioned in the Bible who experienced depression and what worked for them.

The following is written by Pastor Paul Ciniraj, missionary in India, and is worthy of serious contemplation:

WHY SHOULD I...

1. Why should I say I can't when the Bible says I can do all things through Messiah who gives me strength? (Philippians 4:13)

2. Why should I lack when I know that God shall supply all my needs according His riches in glory in Messiah Yeshua? (Philippians 4:19)

3. Why should I fear when the Bible says God has not given me a spirit of fear, but of power, love, and a sound mind? (2 Timothy 1:7)

4. Why should I lack faith to fulfill my calling knowing that God has allotted to me a measure of faith? (Romans 12:3)

5. Why should I be weak when the Bible says that the Lord is the strength of my life and that I will dis-

play strength and take action because I know God? (Psalm 27:1; Daniel 11:32)

6. Why should I allow satan supremacy over my life when He that is in me is greater than he that is in the world? (1 John 4:4)

7. Why should I lack wisdom when Messiah gave wisdom to me from God and God gives wisdom to me generously when I ask for it? (1 Corinthians 1:30; James 1:5)

8. Why should I accept defeat when the Bible says that God always leads me in triumph? (2 Corinthians 2:14)

9. Why should I be depressed when I can recall to mind God's lovingkindness, compassion, and faithfulness and have hope? (Lamentations 3:21-23)

10. Why should I worry and fret when I can cast all my anxiety on Messiah who cares for me? (1 Peter 5:7)

11. Why should I ever be in bondage knowing that there is liberty where the Spirit of the Lord is? (Galatians 5:1)

12. Why should I feel condemned when the Bible says I am not condemned because I am in Messiah? (Romans 8:1)

13. Why should I feel alone when Yeshua said He is with me always, and He will never leave me nor forsake me? (Matthew 28:20; Hebrews 13:5)

14. Why should I feel accursed or a victim of bad luck when the Bible says that Messiah redeemed me from the curse of the law that I might receive His Spirit? (Galatians 3:13-14)

15. Why should I be discontented when I, like Paul, can learn to be content in all my circumstances? (Philippians 4:11)

16. Why should I feel worthless when Messiah became sin on my behalf that I might become the righteousness of God in Him? (2 Corinthians 5:21)

17. Why should I have a persecution complex knowing that nobody can be against me when God is for me? (Romans 8:31)

18. Why should I be confused when God is the author of peace and He gives me knowledge through His indwelling Spirit? (1 Corinthians 14:33, 2:12)

19. Why should I feel like a failure when I am a conqueror in all things through Messiah? (Romans 8:37)

20. Why should I let the pressures of life bother me when I can take courage knowing that Yeshua has overcome the world and its tribulations? (John 16:33)

ABOUT THE AUTHOR

Jeff Zaremsky was born at a very young age. He doubts he was even one day old when he was born. He was so young he hardly remembers it, but his mother insists he was there. When he was eight days old... (well, he would rather not talk about that painful experience right now).

He was very smart in school. His teachers even called him a smart Aleck, even though his name was Jeff not Aleck. He was so smart that the teachers tried to suppress his learning by telling him on more than one occasion, "Don't get smart with me, young man." One teacher was so impressed with his intelligence that she told a substitute, "Keep an eye on that one, he is a wise guy." The principal obviously liked Jeff because he would often invite Jeff to sit in his office with him.

At the age of 19, Jeff started reading the Bible from cover to cover to prove his mother wrong regarding her newfound faith in the Messiah. And that is no joke. In his search he found the Messiah. His only regret was he had not found Him sooner.

In college Jeff minored in humilities (he says he is the humblest person he knows) and majored in apologetics (as a matter of fact he needed to apologize more than any other student or staff in the history of the college). He was offered a Master's of Divinity degree, but he thought it would be a little too much for him to master Divinity (besides that, he doubts God would like being mastered around).

At the age of 26 he met the most wonderful woman who agreed to become his wife. Barbara has put up with Jeff for more than thirty years. Jeff knows that he is special because she often tells him, "You're a real piece of work." When he starts to feel worthless, Barbara reminds him, "You are really something else!"

Today Jeff and Barbara serve two congregations, and direct and edit the *ShalomAdventure.com* website magazine (since he couldn't make it as a comedian).

Jeff has written a few other books including *Jewish Discoveries*, and *Lamentations, the Cry of Hope.*

In the future, Jeff plans on living forever in a new earth thanks to God's wonderful provision and salvation.

Dedication

I dedicate this book to all those who will benefit from it and come out of darkness and into God's glorious light.

ACKNOWLEDGMENTS

First and foremost, I must acknowledge the Lord God Almighty, Creator of Heaven and earth, my Savior, for without Him I can do nothing, yet through Him I can do all things.

A far second, but still extremely important to me, my wonderful wife, Barbara, who truly is one with me.

Also, I want to give thanks to my parents who have been such a blessing to me.

Also, I acknowledge all those who helped proofread the manuscript and/or shared their experiences and stories with me. In no particular order: Kathy Curzon, John and Laurie Trautman, Verna-Lee Small, Erin Parfet, Jennifer Schwirzer, Richard Paracka, Steven Wohlberg, Juanita Kretchmar, Dr. Thom Gardner, Elisa Carothers, and Harmony Jenks.

Experience a personal revival!

Spirit-empowered content from today's top Christian authors delivered directly to your inbox.

Join today!
lovetoreadclub.com

Inspiring Articles
Powerful Video Teaching
Resources for Revival

Get all of this and so much more, e-mailed to you twice weekly!

LOVE TO READ CLUB
by **D DESTINY IMAGE**